Crazy Quilting

THE COMPLETE GUIDE

J. Marsha Michler

This well-embroidered Victorian crazy quilt has a floral theme. Detail.
Museum Collection, Dyer Library/Saco Museum, Saco, Maine.

Published by

kp **krause publications**
An Imprint of F+W Publications
700 East State Street • Iola, WI 54990-0001
715-445-2214 • 888-457-2873
www.krausebooks.com

Our toll-free number to place an order or obtain
a free catalog is (800) 258-0929.

The following trademarked terms and companies appear in this publication:
Caron® Watercolours, DMC® Light Effects, Gloriana, Impressions®, Kreinik Silk
Bella®, Silk Serica®, and Soie Gobelin, Things Japanese, Waterlilies®, Vikki Clayton,
and YLI Cotton Quilting and Pearl Crown Rayon.

Library of Congress Control Number: 2007940515
ISBN-13: 978-0-89689-520-1
ISBN-10: 0-89689-520-3

Designed by Heidi Bittner-Zastrow
Edited by Erica Swanson
Printed in China

Dedication

This book is dedicated to our Victorian-era foremothers,
whose sometimes-impeccable dabbling and always-artful creating
have given us what we have today: the incredible and multi-faceted
art of crazy quilting.

Acknowledgments

First, I'd like to extend my gratitude to all of the wonderful folks at
Krause Publications for seeing yet another of my books into reality. It's
always a pleasure to work with you! Specifically, my thanks to editor Erica
Swanson; book designer Heidi Zastrow; photographer Michael Croatt
(www.wisconsinprairie.com); and acquisitions editor Candy Wiza.
Many thanks to my suppliers and contributors for all of the beautiful
materials that are so fun to use. Your contributions are enrichment to
these pages:

Dena Lenham of Kreinik Mfg. Co., Inc.

Jane Garrison of YLI, Inc.

Vikki Clayton of hand-dyedfibers.com

Maggie Backman of Things Japanese

Ivy Strausberg of The DMC Corporation

Anne Frazier and Gillian Turner of Gloriana Threads

Thanks to Andrea Strassner, curator of the Saco Museum in Saco,
Maine, for permissions to publish photos of the beautiful crazy quilts in
the museum collection.

Thanks to Cindy, Jen, and Sharon of the Limerick Public Library
for showing my work and keeping my books available. Thanks also to
Lisa Ruble of $100,000 Quilting Challenge magazine for publishing my
article on silk crazy quilting (Issue #2, 2007), to Kimber for inviting me to
contribute to CQmag online, and to the students of my Adult Education
crazy quilt class.

A very special thanks to my mom for believing in me all of these
years, and an extra-special thanks to my husband, Gil, for the sushi and
gourmet dinners that have kept this artist sustained.

A Thousand Stitches

Inspired by the idea of creating a book that hones in on the essentials of crazy quilting, a vast concept that will never be conclusive, I designed this quilt with several main ideas.

Quilt style: The oval center is the whole-quilt, while the border consists of the block style of crazy quilting.

Silk fabrics: A celebratory idea, to revel in the luxury of silks! Patches include hand-dyed silks, woven ribbon patches, fabricated patches, pieced fans, and covered buttons.

Embroidery stitches: Stitching along the patch edges is comprised of approximately 1,000 different stitch combinations and variations. Embroidery threads are pulled from my entire stash and include cottons, silks, and rayons of many types.

Embellishments: Techniques and trimmings are cotton and rayon motifs, cotton laces, ribbon work, silk ribbon embroidery, embroidered motifs, photo transfers, covered buttons, and punchneedle.

Design/Contrast: Crazy quilts can be designed with distinctive areas. Contrastive elements in antique crazies tend to be the patches themselves, but here I differentiated by using contrast to define areas.

"A Thousand Stitches"
took second place at the Maine Quilts 2006 show.
The finished quilt is approx. 49" wide by 57" long.

Contents

Introduction

This vintage crazy quilt features beautiful motif embroideries. Detail.
Museum Collection, Dyer Library/Saco Museum, Saco, Maine.

The art quilt of the Victorian Age is revived for modern times with an updated, fresh look but with its roots intact. It is still a means of self expression for needle artists. It still has us gawking over fine fabrics and gorgeous threads; still has us searching for what to do with an old piece of ribbon, or how to dye or paint a piece of cotton lace so it blends into a motif. In a way, little has changed in more than one hundred years.

This book is intended as a reference; that is why projects are featured as examples of techniques without instructions. For project instructions, please refer to my other books and those of other authors.

Use this reference to learn some new skills, hone some beloved old ones, and for suggestions and inspiration. Use these ideas to tweak your quilts and crazy projects with colorful dimension and textures. Enjoy!

What is Crazy Quilting?

Crazy quilting is a creative form of quilting in which patches are made in irregular shapes and sizes. In most methods, patching is worked on a foundation fabric, which displaces the traditional quilt batting. A crazy patched piece is often treated to embroidery and embellishments and is traditionally tied, not running-stitch quilted.

Choose Your Expertise Level

Beginner: Start with cotton muslin foundation, fabrics that hold a crease and are easy to work with, such as cottons, rayons, and linens. Beginners find size 8 pearl cotton the easiest thread for embroidering.

Intermediate: Experiment with incorporating silks and a greater variety of all fabric types. Try other threads, such as rayons and silks, for embroidery. Dabble with all of the embellishment techniques. Be willing to experiment and expand your horizons.

Advanced: Make an all-silk quilt. Use silk organza fabric for a foundation, hand-dyed silk fabrics, and silk threads for embroidery. Work on refining you techniques in any of the embellishment methods.

The Basics

*Fabrics with surface textures
work well for crazy quilting.
Rich texture adds variation to a quilt top or project. Soft prints work nicely, too.*

Fabrics

Rich and varied in their characteristics, fabrics are the background for embroidery and embellishments. Natural fibers are easy to work with and offer wonderful textures. Synthetics are available in many interesting finishes as well. Try them all and pick your favorites. Some of the piecing methods require certain types of fabrics, so check with the method before shopping. See the Appendix for more information about fiber types.

Accumulate a stash, because then you will have plenty of fabric options. Stock up on cottons with interesting weaves, such as damask, sateen, and velveteen; silks such as noil, jacquard, satin, and dupioni; and other fibers, such as lightweight linens and wools, and rayon—especially challis, bridal satins, and taffetas. Also, some lightweight, unbacked upholstery or drapery fabrics offer textures or subtle prints that work well.

Prewash everything that you will use for a washable project. Handwash unless you are sure that all of the fabric is colorfast. If dyes run, keep washing and rinsing until the water runs clear.

Foundations

Most crazy patching methods require a foundation. A plain fabric in a neutral color, such as off-white, works best. The patches are fastened directly onto the foundation, so this fabric becomes a part of the quilt or project. Choose a foundation type according to the type of quilt or project being made. Prewash and press the foundation. As you piece, check often to see that the foundation is staying perfectly smooth with no bunching.

Fabric Options

- **100% cotton muslin:** This is the most common fabric for foundations. It is excellent for quilts, throws, and many other projects. Ease of handling makes it perfect for beginners. Choose high-quality muslins that will keep their shape.

- **100% cotton batiste:** Use batiste for lightweight projects and for quilts and projects (and clothing)

that you want to drape rather than hang flat on a wall. It is softer than muslin and so requires a little extra attention to keep it smooth while patching. The use of a quilter's hoop is a must for embroidery and embellishing.

- **Silk organza:** This type of silk is crispy and perfect for making silk quilts and projects. Use all-silk fabrics to make a featherweight quilt. Buy extra silk organza, because it shrinks significantly when washed.

- **Cotton flannel:** Use flannel as a foundation, or add an extra layer to a quilt for lightweight batting. As a foundation, flannel is soft, so be careful to avoid bunching it.

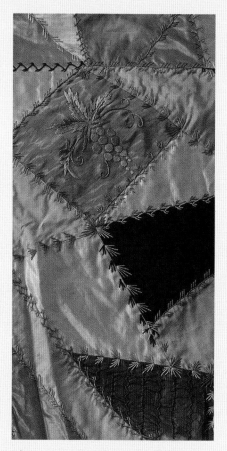

This antique silk quilt features plain-surface fabrics and well-executed patch seam embroidery. Detail. Museum Collection, Dyer Library/Saco Museum, Saco, Maine.

Working with Silk

Silk fabrics give luxury to a crazy quilt unrivaled by other fabric types. Its brilliance of color, weightlessness, interesting surfaces, washability and dye-ability set it apart.

Pair silk with hand-piecing methods, since it is easier to work by hand than by machine. Lightweight silks that otherwise seem to skew all over the place are stabilized by being placed onto a foundation. An all-silk quilt calls for a silk foundation fabric. Use silk organza, and keep it lying flat or it will skew. Square it up on a table or a gridded cutting mat. Use silk pins, or any pins that slide into the fabric without causing fraying. Use a quilter's hoop for embroidery and embellishing.

If there is a lot of static, the air in the room is probably too dry. Add some moisture to the air by spritzing water or using a humidifier.

Press silk using a wool setting. (If the fabric glues itself to the iron, it is a synthetic.)

Dyeing silks is easy (see Silk Dyes, page 195). If you buy one yard each of several different weaves, you can cut them into smaller pieces and dye an unlimited number of colors. Dyeing is a real money-saver that makes silk quilting affordable.

Working with Wool

Wool is adaptable and easy to use for crazy quilting. It is available in weights from drapey challis to thick blankets. For crazy patching, choose weights such as challis or suiting that can be used without becoming too bulky in the seams. Wool loves to be steamed: dampen a press cloth and place it over the fabric, then press lightly. This forces steam into the fabric to flatten it or set a crease.

Wool was used in some crazy quilts in the past (late 1800's and early 1900's). This fabric works out well for crazy quilts, especially since they are tied rather than quilted. Wool fabrics can be embroidered easily with any type of embroidery thread, including wools made for embroidery (knitting yarns may be too thick or too weak). Dimensional embroidery is very attractive in wool threads—use stitches such as Bullion, French Knots and other knots, and Detached Buttonhole.

Consider using the Stained-Glass Method of crazy quilting, especially if you're using felted or thick wool fabrics. This allows you to avoid seam allowances altogether.

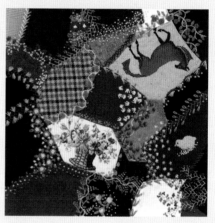

Wool crazy quilts make ideal winter bed coverings. This block features wool patches plus a cross stitch on linen, and a piece of needlepoint used as patches. Embroidery is done in wool threads.

Color

Working with color can be the most challenging aspect of any type of quilting.

In any arrangement, use lots of neutrals. Black is common in many antique crazy quilts and serves to highlight surrounding colors. It is especially attractive in jewel-tone quilts. Browns are excellent colors in crazy quilts also. They come in many shades from chocolate to taupe to rust. Brown is compatible with almost any scheme. Creams and off-whites are great backgrounds for embroideries.

Jewel-tone schemes are found in many antique crazy quilts. These include a range of brilliant colors such as red, green, purple, and gold.

Often, color schemes are chosen by simply choosing a range of colors that appear compatible with each other. This is a fine way to pick colors if your combinations are satisfying to you. If your color senses fail you however, look for a good

Reds from mid-tone to burgundy, yellows, and plenty of browns predominate the color scheme of this vintage crazy quilt. The colors are mainly warm shades with some blues. Detail. Museum Collection, Dyer Library/Saco Museum, Saco, Maine.

color reference and study it. There are books for working with color in painting, other arts, and quilting. Any of these will reveal useful information for using colors in a crazy quilt. It can be especially helpful to carefully analyze the colors in quilts or other works that are attractive to you. Along with a study of color theory, this will sharpen your color senses.

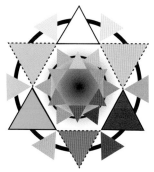

This mandala is a color wheel. Creating a color wheel of your own is a great way to begin to learn about colors. The three "primary" or basic colors are yellow, blue, and red. The basic colors are considered "pure," because there are no mixtures that can create them.

Three secondary colors are made by mixing the primary ones together: orange (red and yellow), violet (red and blue), and green (blue and yellow).

The tertiary colors are those shown between the primary and the secondary colors in the outer ring of the wheel.

In the outer ring of the wheel, the colors are pure. If any of these are mixed with white, they become lighter (pastel), but still remain pure. The inner ring shows shaded colors, those mixed with a speck of black. This makes the shades grayer and creates muted tones. Not shown on the wheel are browns. These are derived by mixing various combinations of the pure colors.

The Color Wheel

Create color schemes derived from the color wheel.

Monochromatic: Using various shades of one color; this is the simplest type of color scheme.

Analogous: Colors with shared characteristics (next to each other on the wheel). Analogous color schemes are easy and harmonious.

Complementary: Two colors that have no shared characteristics. On the color wheel, they are opposites. These opposites used together create vibrancy.

Cool colors: Those on the blue side of the wheel.

Warm colors: Those on the red to yellow side of the wheel.

A color scheme can consist of only cool or warm colors, or be a blend of each.

Greyed tones: Those toward the center of the wheel.

Above all, try not to foster any color prejudices. It is an interesting experiment to work with those colors that you think you dislike, or those that you haven't used. It will stimulate the creative part of your brain and open you up to new possibilities!

Design in Crazy Quilting

Concepts of design drawn from the art world readily apply to crazy quilting. These include pattern (repetition), balance, contrast, and unity. It is important to pay attention to the composition of your project. Your own intuition will tell you whether you need to do some design research.

Pay attention to how much you see in the world around you. A lot of art comes from our own perceptions: how we see things. Are you noticing patterns? Shadows? A small scene or still-life that could make an interesting embroidery? The inherent colorfulness of an apparently bland object, such as a stone? Some good books on this topic, or a college-level art appreciation course can be helpful to unlock your creativity.

Tools

Basic hand-working tools include fabric shears, embroidery scissors, sewing needles, embroidery needles, and pins. Quality counts, especially where cutting is concerned.

Be sure to keep all-metal shears and scissors honed. You can do this yourself if instructions came with the scissors. If a scissors has a knife edge, honing needs to be done a certain way so you do not ruin the cutting edge. All-metal scissors also operate easily, putting no strain on your hands.

Use a separate scissors for cutting paper. Paper dulls a good fabric scissors.

An iron is essential. Close work, such as pressing under the edges of patches, requires a dry iron so you don't burn your fingers. I never put water in my iron, and I keep a spray bottle handy in case I do need steam. Use a press cloth in case pressing leaves a shine on the fabric or spray causes spotting (spray the press cloth instead of the fabric).

A sewing machine is needed for some of the piecing methods, machine embellishments, and for finishing a quilt. You will need a plain machine that does straight stitching and zigzag. A treadle or a Singer Featherweight is fine too—you can get by without zigzag.

Some piecing methods require a cutting mat, rotary cutter, and acrylic ruler. Invest in a good-sized cutting mat. Mine is 36" x 24", and I use it for piecing, basting a hand-pieced quilt top (it prevents marring desktops and tabletops), and cutting bias strips for bindings.

Workspace

How your work area is set up is important, because it is easier to work on a project if you can do so efficiently. You will also be more likely to use your space if it is attractive and organized.

Excellent lighting is essential. Compact fluorescent bulbs fit into many kinds of light fixtures. They allow you to see the colors and are easier on the eyes than incandescent bulbs. It isn't necessary to invest in expensive color-corrected bulbs—instead, pick your fabric and thread colors using natural daylight, and then work with any kind of light. Task lights and gooseneck lamps allow you to redirect the light as needed for close work at a sewing machine or for doing handwork in an easy chair.

For hand patching, piece the foundation directly on an ironing board. If the foundation is large, place the ironing board next to a table or desk to keep it flat. For machine work, place the ironing board beside your

sewing desk and lower it so you can sew, then press easily.

Storage is just as important as work space. It's a lot easier to get things done if you can find what you need. Use boxes, bins, shelves, dressers, cabinets, and drawers to keep your things organized.

Ten Ways to Patch a Crazy Quilt

The blocks in this vintage crazy quilt appear to have been patched using the Antique Method (see page 20).

Museum Collection, Dyer Library/Saco Museum, Saco, Maine.

Hand-worked embroidery stitches bring a patched block to the next level. Note how the block has changed from the patched and basted step (step 2). Embroidery adds vibrant detail while allowing the patches to visually meld together.

Threads are DMC Size 8 Pearl Cottons.

The by-hand Antique method is as old as vintage Victorian crazy quilts. Nothing throughout the passage of time has improved upon it. It is artful, creative, and offers flexibility in the process. The method begins by laying patches onto a foundation. This not only seems "painterly" to do, but also makes it easy to view how the color scheme is working and to make changes before anything is fastened down. After patching, the overlapped edges of patches are pressed under and basted. The unsewn edges have dimension and a kind of natural look that is retained even after they are ultimately fastened in place with embroidery stitches. Hand patching, furthermore, makes it easy to incorporate patches with curved edges. This lends a softening effect to the composition in its entirety that is characteristic of the most beautiful of the Victorian crazy quilts.

The sizes to make both the foundation and the patches are individual preference. A foundation can be the size of the entire quilt top, or a block of any size. If you are planning to work embroideries or embellishments on the centers of patches, make the patches an appropriate size.

Pros: Artful, creative, and flexible: patches can be rearranged before they are fastened into place. It is easy to make curved-edge patches. Results are a softer look, as well as greater dimensionality than machine-sewn patches.

Considerations: Patches must be fastened in place by embroidery.

Materials:

Muslin or other foundation fabric, cotton thread for basting, variety of fabric scraps for patches, your choice of embroidery threads and embellishments.

Tools:

Fabric shears, pins, dry iron, sewing needle. Embroidery scissors and needles.

Instructions:

Overlap patches at least ½" to allow for ¼" or greater seam allowances. Cut the foundation to the size needed plus seam allowances. Cut each patch as it is needed. Have the foundation on a flat surface.

1 Cut a patch-sized piece of fabric and pin it in place. You can begin at a corner or anywhere on the foundation.

2 Continue to cut and add patches until the foundation is covered. Be sure they are overlapped by at least ½". Pin each as it is laid.

3 One patch at a time, unpin and press under the seam allowances of overlapped edges. Re-pin. If desired, add laces and trims along the patch edges and meandering across the patches. Pin them in place.

4 Hand baste along the folded edges of the patches and along trims. Baste around the entire foundation.

5 Work embroidery along the edges of the patches. Remove the basting.

This block has a mostly-green color scheme with a complementary dash of red.

Embroidery stitches portray roses and bugs.

Embroidery threads are hand-dyed silks from Gloriana.

Read through the information on the Antique method, because much of it applies here. The difference between the methods is that here, the patch edges are pressed under at the same time the patches are laid. To be sure that patches will fit together easily, cut most of them with curved or widely angled edges.

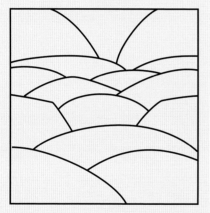

It is easy to create beautiful landscapes with this method. Forming hills, oceans, or skies is intuitive. For example, to make the effect of rolling hills, cut most of the patches with a rounded edge. To create perspective, make farther away patches smaller and lighter or grayer in color.

Pros: This method is similar to the Antique method. It is easy to create landscapes.

Considerations: The similarity in patches can appear monotonous. For variety, turn the block and patch from all directions. Patches must be fastened in place with embroidery.

Materials:
Muslin or other foundation fabric
Variety of scrap fabrics for patches
Embroidery threads
Basting thread
Laces and trims (optional)

Tools:
Fabric shears, pins, dry iron, sewing needle, embroidery scissors, and needles

Instructions:

1 Cut the foundation fabric to the size needed plus seam allowances.

2 Cut a patch with a rounded edge. Press the rounded edge under at least ¼". Lay the patch in one corner. Pin.

3 Cut a second patch. Press under the edge(s) that will be overlapped, and lay it on the foundation. Tuck the raw edge of the second patch under the previous patch.

4 Add a third patch, repeating step 2. You will see that the only edges left unfinished are at the edges of the block. Repeat until the foundation is covered.

5 Add any laces or trims that will be sewn into the seams.

6 Hand baste along the folded edges of the patches, being sure to stitch over the trims to hold them in place. Baste around the entire foundation.

7 Work embroidery along the edges of the patches. Remove the basting thread.

2

3

4
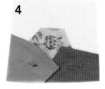

5

6

A machine method, Confetti Piecing results in skewed "patches."
This is a completely random method that is very easy to do.

This by-machine method consists of piecing, and is entirely random. It is easier than other methods because you can happily cut and sew. Don't be fooled by lengthy instructions—the method is easier than it looks!

Traditional quilting cotton fabrics are easiest to use, and they work best for learning the method. If you choose other types of fabrics, be sure they are stable (not inclined to shift or stretch). Instructions call for eight different prints and solids, but you can use as few as four, or as many as you like.

Place a foundation fabric on the back of a sewn piece in order to do machine or hand embroidery on it. See "Muted Joys in Cloth" in the gallery section for an example of both machine and hand embroidery on a confetti-pieced background.

Or, more traditionally, add some batting and a backing, and machine quilt the layers. Finish by binding the edges (see page 245). This is a great way to make a quilt in a hurry.

Pros: This is a simple, fast method that makes use of familiar cotton fabrics. Confetti Piecing results in a more random look than the Right Sides Together method.

Considerations: The seams are all angular.

Materials:
8 lengths (¼ yd. each) of cotton quilting fabrics in a mix of prints and solids
Sewing thread

Tools:
Sewing machine, rotary cutter, cutting mat, acrylic ruler, and iron

Instructions:

1 Stack the eight quarter-yard lengths of fabric evenly, and cut about 5" from the end of the stack. Press seams to one side as each is sewn.

2 Sew the pieces into two blocks of four.

3 Using the rotary cutter, cutting mat, and acrylic ruler, make a diagonal cut across one of the blocks.

4 Place one of the diagonally-cut pieces onto the uncut block, placing it diagonally. Cut along the previously cut edge.

5 Make two new blocks by aligning the diagonally cut edges. Pin, and sew. You can see now how the pieces are starting to "jumble."

6 Decide where to make the next cut (you can make it anywhere you like). Make the cut and reassemble the pieces to form two new blocks, as

in step 5. Continue to do this until the blocks are as "jumbled" as you want them to be.

7 Lastly, sew the two blocks together to form one large block.

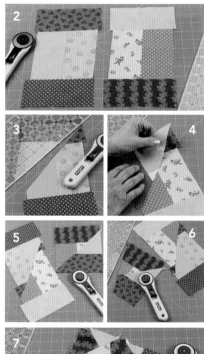

Self-made cordings and hand-dyed silk ribbons provide much of the decor on this block.

Embroidery threads are from the Caron Collection.

If you have sewn garments or done patchwork, you may find this method more intuitive than others. This is because patches are machine sewn with right sides together.

Sometimes this method can result in an unattractive "skewed Log Cabin quilting" look, consisting of straight-edged triangular pieces spiraling out from a central core. But with just a pinch of extra thought, you can avoid this effect. Add some curved-edge patches, and use the tip on the next page.

Pros: Patches are sewn in place as they are added.

Considerations: Patches cannot be rearranged without ripping out seams. Patching has a tendency to resemble skewed Log Cabin quilting.

Materials:
Muslin or other foundation fabric
Variety of scrap fabrics for patches
Embroidery threads and embellishments
Sewing thread

Tools:
Fabric shears, pins, iron, sewing machine, embroidery scissors, and needles

Instructions:
1 Cut the foundation to the size needed plus seam allowances.

2 Cut a patch and lay it (facing up) anywhere on the foundation. (Each patch will be cut as it is needed.) Add laces and other trims that will be sewn into the seams. Cut a second patch, and lay it with right sides together on the first. Pin.

3 Sew the seam. Each time a patch is sewn on, trim the seam allowances to about ¼". Open out the second patch and press.

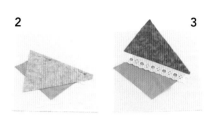

2   **3**

4 The third patch here is being laid as in the Antique method. Cut the patch with a rounded edge. Press the rounded edge under and lay the patch in place. Pin.

4   **5**

5 Cut and add a fourth patch the same as in steps 1 and 2.

6 Add patches until the block is covered. Baste the curved edge of the piece added in step 3. Baste around the outer edge of the block.

6

7 Work embroidery along the patch seams. Remove basting.

TIP Sew several patches together to make a larger patch before sewing onto the foundation. The fourth patch consists of three pieces that are sewn together, then added to the foundation.

If you get into a bind and need two seams instead of one, machine sew one seam and appliqué the other. The fifth patch must be added this way.

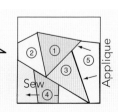

Strip Patching

Most of the fabrics in this piece are cottons. Cotton fabrics are easy to work with and offer great surface texture, including prints that appear to be textured. Embroidery threads are DMC Pearl cotton, with Kreinik metallics adding a sparkly touch.

It is relatively simple to crazy patch a narrow foundation, making this method great for beginners. It is perfect for making bell pulls, such as the one shown in the Gallery. Sew long, strip-pieced pieces side by side to form a quilt, or use them as borders or sashings in a quilt. See Styles of Crazy Quilts on page 228 for ideas.

The technique is the same as the Right Sides Together method. The only difference is that it is worked along the length of a strip of foundation fabric instead of a block. Refer to that method for adding curved edge patches. In the instructions, a wide piece of eyelet lace is used as a patch.

Pros: Strip Patching is very easy to do. This method is great for silk fabrics (see the Blue Silk Bell Pull on page 56).

Considerations: A quilt with this method takes on a strip format.

Materials:

Muslin for foundation
Scrap fabrics for patches
Sewing thread
Embroidery threads and
embellishments

Tools:

Fabric shears, pins, iron, sewing
machine, embroidery scissors, and
needles

2

3

4

Instructions:

1 Cut the foundation to the length
and width needed plus seam allowances. For example, the foundation
in the following examples is cut 4"
wide and will finish to 3½" with ¼"
seam allowances.

2 Place the first patch at one end.
Here, a piece of lace has been
added to be sewn into the seam.

3 Cut a second patch to the
approximate shape desired plus
seam allowances. Place it with right
sides together onto the first patch,
pin and sew. Open out and press.

4 Continue to add patches until the
foundation is covered.

5 Embroider by hand or machine as
you like.

The decoration on this block includes metallic self-made cordings,
brass charms, and tiny mother-of-pearl buttons.

Threads are silks from Gloriana.

This is a useful method where you may want to fit patches into an area in a certain way, or for beginners who don't have the confidence to cut patches randomly. The "Crazy Altered Book" (see page 57) was designed using this method so that individual shapes could be cut out of cardboard before being finished with fabric.

Different patch shapes are featured throughout this book. You can also sketch lines on paper to create your own design. If you are making several blocks that will be joined together, you may want to make a different pattern for each block. Otherwise, use different fabrics on each, and turn them in different directions to differentiate them.

Pros: Any guesswork is eliminated.

Considerations: Extra steps make this method take longer to do.

Materials:

See method to be used, and step 5 below. Use the Right Sides Together method (see page 29), the Antique method (see page 20), or English Paper Piecing (see page 37)

Tools:

See method to be used, and step 5 on the next page. Plain paper, tracing paper, pencil, ruler, and scissors

Instructions:

1 Draw the design for the patched block on a sheet of paper (seam allowances are not added at this point).

1

2 Trace the design. Cut out the traced patch pieces and place them in order on a flat surface.

3
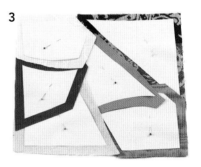

3 One patch at a time, lay the pattern piece on a piece of fabric and cut around, adding at least a ¼" seam allowance.

4 Cut a piece of foundation fabric the size of the block plus seam allowances.

5

5 Use the Right Sides Together method (see page 29), the Antique method (see page 20), or English Paper Piecing (following) to sew the patches in place.

6 Embroider.

English Paper Piecing

English Paper Piecing is a means of joining the patches, making use of the paper pattern pieces. This method does not give the solid support of a foundation. If you will be working embroidery, baste the sewn block onto a foundation.

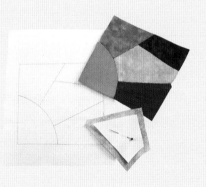

1 Use freezer paper. Iron the coated side onto the wrong side of the fabric. Cut out each pattern piece so the coated side faces right-side up. (see step 2).

2 Take one pattern piece and place it right-side down onto the wrong side of a piece of fabric. (Both are wrong-side up).

3 Cut around, adding a seam allowance of approximately ¼" on all sides.

4 Press the edges of the fabric to the back of the paper pattern piece.

5 Invisibly hand stitch two adjoining pieces together. Continue to sew the pieces to each other until the block is sewn. When finished, remove the papers.

The Collage method can take a heavy dose of machine work, with or without hand embroidery. Here, YLI Variegated quilting thread secures the pieces.
Touches of hand embroidery are worked in YLI silk ribbon and DMC Pearl cotton.

This incredibly simple and creative method can give two entirely different results, depending on your approach. Follow the instructions to create a crazy patched look. See below for the free-form version.

The method is as simple as layering or piling fabrics, trims, and threads onto a foundation and then machine sewing over it until everything is held in place. It is designed to be sewn entirely by machine, although touches of hand work may be added later.

Pick one or more interesting threads for sewing the layers. There are many machine-sewing threads available for creating various effects. Choose from silks and rayons in matte or glossy finishes, metallic and fibrous synthetics, or 100% cotton quilting thread in a range of colors. Threads that are too heavy for the machine may be couched by zigzag stitching (see Couching on page 221).

Choose a firm fabric, such as a sturdy muslin or even a heavy interfacing for the foundation. If the foundation tends to buckle as you sew, add a stabilizer underneath. For extra loft, place a layer of batting on top of the foundation.

Pros: This is the easiest method of all.

Considerations: Large projects may be too tedious, since they require lots of machine stitching.

Materials:

Foundation fabric
Fabric scraps
Trims
Sewing threads
Batting (optional)
Stabilizer (optional)

Tools:

Sewing machine (you may need a denim needle if you have thick layers), fabric shears, pins, embroidery scissors, and needles

Instructions:

1 Cut the foundation fabric to the size needed plus seam allowances. Add a layer of batting, if desired.

2 Cut the fabrics into patch-sized pieces. Arrange them on top of the foundation or batting, right-side up, without turning the edges under. Pin them in place.

3 Add some trims, pinning them also. They do not need to be pinned exactly in place because they will be shaped as they are sewn.

4 Machine sew the trims in place, and then sew random, curved, or straight lines anywhere on the piece. Change thread colors as desired. Continue sewing until everything is held in place. Ravel and fluff the exposed fabric edges.

5 Add some hand embroidery, if desired.

2

3

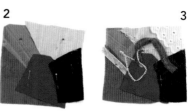

4

Freeform Collage

This is a great way to use up small trimmings without using patches. Pile small cuttings of fabrics, ribbons, and threads onto a sturdy foundation, and then machine stitch as in step 3 above. Add additional embellishment, such as silk ribbon embroidery and beading, if desired. The finished piece can be squared up, glued onto heavy paper, and used as a greeting card or postcard.

Topstitch Appliqué

This block is embroidered entirely in glass seed beads in embroidery-like formations.

Topstitch Appliqué is a machine method that makes it easy to use patches with curved edges. Sewing a trim over the edge of a patch both secures the trim and finishes the edge.

Depending on the trims, the finished effect can be very decorative. Because of this, hand or machine embroidery may not be needed. For a "wedding cake" look, choose all-white fabrics and trims.

Pros: Patches are sewn in place and embellished with one line of stitching.

Considerations: Some planning is required to sew the patch edges.

Materials:

Muslin or other foundation fabric
Variety of scrap fabrics for patches
Trims with finished edges
Embroidery threads
Matching thread
Cotton thread for basting

Tools:

Fabric shears, pins, iron, sewing machine, embroidery scissors, and needles

Instructions:

1 Cut the foundation fabric to the size needed plus seam allowances. Use a stabilizer underneath if the fabrics do not lie smooth while you sew.

2

2 Cut a patch with a rounded edge to fit into a corner, and lay it in place. Pin.

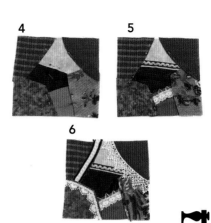

3 Make a second patch to fit under the first so the edges are overlapped by at least 1". Continue to add patches in the same way. Pin each as it is added.

4 Press under ½" of each overlapped edge.

5 Find the most underlapped patch and pin a trim along its edge. Conceal the ends of the trim under adjoining patches. Placing the line of stitching about ¼" in from the fold, sew the trim in place.

6 Continue, finding the most underlapped patch each time (if you don't, you will be opening up seams later).

7 Add some hand embroidery if desired.

4

5

6

Basted Appliqué Variation

The purple thread basting will be taken out as hand embroidery is added. The fabrics are pieces of old kimonos. A selection of embroidery materials include Kreinik's Japan thread and braid, and a Gloriana silk thread.

Follow instructions for Topstitch Appliqué, but eliminate the sewn trim and sew a line of machine basting instead. Patch edges only need to be turned under ¼" instead of ½". Hand embroider over the basting. Remove the basting.

The only decor needed on this two-sided piece are the frayed edges of the patches.

This block was sewn using YLI Variegated quilting thread.

This method creates finished surfaces on both front and back of the work, making the project two-sided. Patch edges are not turned under. There is no foundation, and the resulting piece is not backed, so technically it is not a form of quilting—but is crazy piecing, nonetheless.

Use the Two-sided Topstitch Appliqué method to make lightweight, durable afghans. Choose fabrics that ravel easily and are machine washable. These include light upholstery, drapery, or pants-weight fabrics. This is a great way to use up worn denim jeans! For a bright touch, sew the afghan using a contrasting thread. Finish the afghan by machine washing and drying to fray the edges.

This method is ideal for making lace curtains or table coverings. Use all-over lace fabrics and cotton batiste. Sew pintucks, tucks, and pleats in batiste to create textured fabrics. Sew laces or ribbons together to create fabrics. Refer to a book about heirloom sewing for more information on these techniques.

There are a number of ways to finish the edges of an afghan or lace piece. Bind with bias binding (see page 245), turn under and hem, or sew on a purchased fringe or trim.

Pros: This method is very easy, and it is reversible, so it doesn't require a foundation.

Considerations: Although it is crazy quilting-related, it is not technically quilting since there is only one layer of fabric.

Materials:

Machine-washable heavy cotton or cotton-type fabric scraps, or lace and batiste fabric

Laces and trims

Cotton sewing thread

Tools:

Sewing machine with zigzag stitches, fabric shears, and pins

2

3

Instructions:

1 Set your sewing machine to do a zigzag stitch about 2 mm wide (or use a different width to suit your fabric and preference), with a stitch length that is short and yet allows the work to move along at a respectable pace. Use the same thread in the top as in the bobbin.

2 Cut a patch with a rounded edge. Lay it onto a second piece of fabric.

3 For an afghan, zigzag about ¼" in from the rounded edge of the patch. Sew a second row of zigzag about ⅜" in from the first. To sew lace, sew a line of straight stitching using a short stitch length. Trim the lace up to the stitching, and then sew a row of zigzag over the stitching and the raw edge. Sew a second row the same as above.

4 Turn the work over, and trim the second patch (up to ¼" of the stitching for an afghan and up to the stitching for lace). Remember to do this step each time you add a patch.

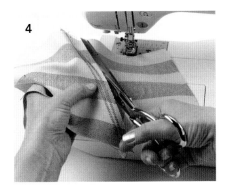

5 Add the next patch the same way as the first.

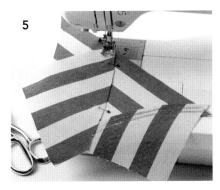

6 Add patches until the piece is the size needed. Square up the edges, and finish them as desired.

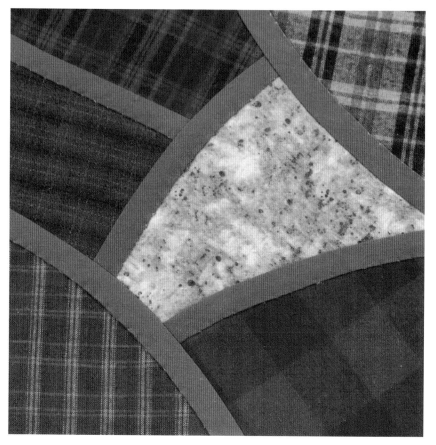

Yes, you can crazy quilt with cotton flannel fabrics! This method allows you to avoid bulky seams while adding a uniting touch between prints.

The Stained-Glass Method offers a neat way to finish the edges of patches: cover them with bias strips instead of turning them under. You can use fabrics such as flannel or even blanket-weight wool without creating fat seams.

Fabrics that work best are those that stay in place when you lay them on the foundation. This includes cotton flannels, other cottons, and wool.

Embroidery and embellishment are optional. The Tote Bag in the Gallery (see page 61) is an example of hand work with the Stained Glass method. The method can be done with a machine or by hand.

To work by hand, substitute hand sewing in step 6, leaving the bias tape edge folded under. Handstitch invisibly.

Pros: A "stained-glass" effect is produced. This method is ideal for some fabrics that are difficult to use in other methods.

Considerations: Requires using fabrics that will stay in place on the foundation until they are sewn down.

Materials:

Muslin fabric for foundation
Fabrics for patches, such as flannel or lightweight wool
Smooth cotton fabric for bias strips
Sewing thread.

Tools:

Sewing machine (optional), fabric shears, pins, sewing needle, bias tape maker for ½"-wide bias.

Instructions:

1 Cut the smooth cotton fabric into bias strips 1⅛" wide (see Bias Binding on page 245). You will need enough to cover all of the patch seams, so make a best guess to figure out how much to cut. Press the long edges under using a bias tape maker, if you have one. The finished pieces should be ½" wide or a little more. Cut the foundation to the desired size.

2 Cut a patch with a rounded edge to fit into one corner of the foundation. Pin.

3 Cut a second patch and fit it under the edge of the first. Pin. Cut along the edge of the first patch and remove the excess fabric from underneath.

4 Continue to cut and lay patches the same as in step 2 until the foundation is covered. All cut edges will be butted together with no underlapping or overlapping.

5 Find the "most underlapped" patch. This means you will not have to open up seams that have already been sewn. Open out one edge of the bias tape, and lay the fold line of the tape ¼" in from the edge of the patch. Trim the ends to fit the length of the seam.

6 Machine sew along the foldline of the opened out bias tape, then fold

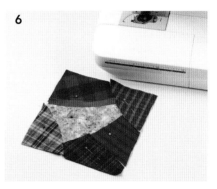

the tape over the seam and press. Continue with steps 4 and 5 until all seams are covered.

7 Hand sew the remaining edges invisibly.

The craft of crazy quilting presents a wide range of wondrous opportunities for making different styles and types of quilts (refer to my book, *Crazy Quilts by Machine*, for quilt design ideas) and other projects. Each item in this Gallery illustrates one of the piecing methods from the previous chapter.

Working in Miniature

Some of the projects shown are worked in miniature. This means the finished piece is a typically large size thing made much smaller. A quilt in a size suitable for a pendant is a drastic reduction in size, while a small-size quilt is less so. Patches can be made smaller than normal, and often embroidery materials and stitches can be downsized also.

A small format is a great way to experiment: with color schemes, border ideas, quilt styles, or to try a patching method.

Working in small scale is not as difficult as it may seem. Choose fabrics that are easy to manage in small pieces. Many silks work beautifully for this purpose. Choose embellishment and embroidery materials that complement the scale of the piece.

The Antique Method

This all-silk mini quilt was designed with a circular center and corner fans. It was embroidered with Silk Serica threads on hand-dyed and commercially dyed silk fabrics. Techniques include punchneedle, silk ribbon embroidery, trapunto, and motif embroideries.

Approx. 13" square

Beaded Pendant on Copper

The Landscape Method

Very small pieces of hand-dyed silk fabrics create blue sky behind autumn-colored foothills enhanced with glass seed beads. The landscape was embroidered with Silk Bella thread and Kreinik metallics. Self-made hanging cord of rayon ribbon, Pearl Crown Rayon thread, DMC Rayon floss, and Kreinik copper metallic braid gives the pendant texture. The pendant was backed with sheet copper and finished with a soldered-on copper bail.

Approx. 2¼" square

The Confetti Method

Projects can take on a personality of their own as you create them. For me, this one expresses a kind of joy on a laid-back day, seemingly oxymoronic but not really. Confetti pieced cotton quilting fabrics (solids and subtle prints) are a background for splashes of machine quilting and hand embroidery. The quilt includes self-made cording and a silk ribbon commercial trim. It was quilted with YLI Cotton Quilting thread and embroidered with DMC Pearl Cotton and YLI silk ribbon.

15" wide by 18¾" long

Antique-Looking Purse

Right Sides Together Method

Achieve the look of antiquity by using "browned" colors, mottled hand dyes, and old buttons. This purse was sewn with the Right Sides Together method out of silk fabrics, some hand dyed and one hand painted. The button closure is a tarnished antique. A heavily glass-beaded fringe adds sparkle. Embellishments include embroidery with Silk Serica and Impressions threads, Kreinik metallics, hand-dyed chenille, silk ribbons, seed beads, genuine amethyst, and glass beads.

Approx. 9¼" wide by 7¾" long, not including handle

Strip Piecing Method

Two bells have their own openings (use the Inset technique on page 225), and four are tied into the rayon fringe. Hand dyed silks and shaped-edge patches, trapunto, and other fabrications from the machine methods part of this book contributed to the bell pull. It was embroidered with Kreinik braids, ribbons and facets; YLI Pearl Crown Rayon; and YLI Silk Ribbon. Additional embellishments include antiqued brass bells, a handmade tassel (see page 164) "tied" with wire, and hand-formed brass wire hanging hardware.

4½" wide by 22" long,
not including tassel

Crazy Altered Book

Make a Pattern Method

An altered book is an existing book that is changed in various ways by the artist. To do a similar, crazy piece book cover, first draw up the design. Cut the "patches" out of cardboard. Cover each cardboard piece first with batting, and then with silk fabric brought to the back and glued. Glue them to the book cover. Use metallic paint, brass wires, rhinestones, and a crystal button to decorate.

Approx. 5¼" wide by 10¼" long

Collage Method

Because patch edges are left raw, the Collage Method creates a textural surface different from other forms of crazy quilting. Machine sewn patches and trims provide background to handwork (added last). Made of silk and silk/rayon fabrics with ribbonwork, silk ribbon embroidery, and beading. Kreinik metallic braids and ribbons, rayon ribbons, self-made cordings. Sewn with YLI quilting thread.

13½" square

Especially When the October Wind

Topstitch Appliqué Method

Inspired by Dylan Thomas' poem, this quilt is a study in reds, an experiment with fans (half circle in place of the usual quarter circle), and a glorying in the richness of patterned silk fabrics. Fat Silk Serica threads contradict the miniaturism of the quilt. Silk Serica, Silk Bella, Soie Gobelin, Waterlilies threads, and YLI silk ribbons were used to create the quilt.

Approx. 14" square

Table Runner

Two-sided Topstitch Appliqué Method

Yes, you can crazy quilt lace curtains; this table runner proves it. This lovely runner is made from 100% cotton batiste fabric, cotton and nylon laces, and trims. It is edged with a pleated eyelet ruffle topped with rayon Venice trim.

Approx. 17" wide by 58" long.

Tote Bag

Stained-Glass Method

It's fun to make something funky and carry it everywhere. And if your tote bag gets you compliments, you must be doing something right! Designed, without a pattern, to fit the handles, the tote is created from flannels and decorating fabric using machine stitching, hand embroidery, self-made cording, and lots of added details. I used YLI Quilting thread and DMC Size 8 Pearl cotton.

Approx. 15" wide by 11" long, not including handles.

Faux Crazy Quilting

Crazy quilting that is mimicked in materials other than fabrics can be called "faux" or false crazy quilting. Here it is in needlepoint, used to make a cover for a spiral notebook. "Windows" worked in the needlepoint showcase small brass wire pieces. The needlepoint is worked in Paternayan Persian wool yarn, YLI Light Effects metallic threads, and The Caron Collection Watercolours. Embroidery stitches are in YLI Pearl Crown Rayon thread. The cover features pockets in the interior flaps and a hook-and-loop tape closure.

The needlepoint area is 9¾" x 6¾"

Embroidery by Hand

If there is one thing that sets crazy quilts apart from other kinds of quilts, it is hand embroidery. Embroidery along patch seams softens angularities, creates dimension and texture, and gives incredible character to a quilt or project.

This antique silk quilt features a variety of embroidery stitches along patch edges. Detail. Museum Collection, Dyer Library/Saco Museum, Saco, Maine.

Purchase the best-quality tools you can afford.

- Embroidery scissors: All-metal scissors for trimming small areas of fabrics, ripping out unwanted stitches, and cutting threads.
- Embroidery needles: Have assorted sizes on hand.
- Milliner's (straw) needles: Buy assorted sizes also; these needles are best for doing the Bullion stitch because the wraps will easily slide off the needle.

- Size 18 chenille needles: These are for embroidering with silk ribbons. Use for metal threads and chenille as well.
- Embroidery hoop: Use a 6" hoop for small areas and a 4" hoop for even smaller areas. I like to use hoops for filling in motif embroideries and for punchneedle.
- 14" quilter's lap hoop: This is an essential tool that frees up both hands so it is easier (and quicker) to embroider. The quilter's lap hoop is excellent for beading, couching, and silk ribbon embroidery, as well as embroidery stitching along patch seams. If your project is smaller than the hoop, enlarge it by sewing panels of scrap fabric to the edges of the project (you don't need multiple sizes of hoops that way).

Threads

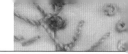

The threads shown on the following pages are only a representative selection. Creatively hand-dyed threads are wonderful for crazy quilt embroidery. Try as many types as you can to find your favorites. When you do, it often makes sense to buy the entire range of colors offered. Then you will not be missing "just the right color."

Other embroidery materials include silk ribbons; metallic threads, braids, and ribbons; and miscellaneous fibers and yarns, some of which can be sewn through fabric, and others that must be couched.

Twisted threads are recommended for embroidery along patch seams. They are not embroidery flosses and are not separated into strands. Floss tends to flatten out while twisted threads stay dimensional once embroidered. This gives beautiful surface texture to your project.

Different Types of Threads

Size 8 pearl (perle) cotton is a standard for crazy quilting. Size 5 is heavier, and 12 is finer.

Threads for motif embroideries within patches include the flosses. Not shown are cotton flosses, which are very common. Flosses are made to be separated into individual strands. Use a single strand for very fine work.

Ribbons for embroidery are available in two basic types. One is woven for the purpose of embroidery, and the other is silk yardage cut on the bias. The bias-cut silk ribbons have unfinished edges. Either type can be found beautifully hand-dyed in a wide range of colors. If you prefer, you can easily hand dye your own ribbons (see Silk Dyes, page 195).

> **TIP** When a quilt top is gaining in embellishments, wrap the stationary one of the two hoops with a soft fabric, such as batiste or gauze. A few stitches in the end of the wraps holds them in place. This provides padding for the embellishments.

Twisted threads include DMC, Needle Necessities, Paternayan Persian, and Gloriana wools. YLI rayon thread. Cottons are from The Caron Collection and Needle Necessities. Silks are from Kreinik, Gloriana, and Things Japanese.

Flosses by Caron Collection, Au Ver A Soie, Needle Necessities, Kreinik, DMC, Vikki Clayton, and Gloriana.

Ribbons by YLI, Vikki Clayton, Artemis, Things Japanese, and Gloriana.

Metallics add glitz to your projects. Some metallic threads can be threaded into the sewing machine, and others can be used for hand embroidery. Heavier metallic threads, narrow ribbons, and braids can be couched by hand or machine. "Japans" are thin pieces of metal wrapped around a fiber core. Japans are mainly used in silk and metal embroideries, but they can be used in crazy quilting as well. Hand couch them using fine silk thread.

Assorted fibers for embroidery and embellishment include chenilles often seen on Victorian crazy quilts. This photo only shows a small selection. There are many variety yarns available that can be used in the same way. Couch them by hand or machine (see Couching, page 221).

Metallics by Kreinik, YLI, DMC, and Things Japanese.

Chenille and good variety yarns by Quilter's Resource, YLI, Needle Necessities, Caron and Vikki Clayton.

- Needles wear out. Buy extra and discard them when the point starts to get rough or the eye causes fraying.
- Cut an appropriate length of thread. If the thread wears or frays easily (silks, rayons, and metallics), use about 18"; use up to a yard for smooth cottons.
- When using delicate threads, instead of "sewing," pull the thread all the way through to make each part of the stitch.
- Twisted silk threads sometimes appear to disintegrate. If that happens, slide the needle down the thread to where it comes through the fabric. Run the thread upwards through your fingers, repeating until the plies run evenly. Bring up the needle, and continue stitching.

- When using more than one strand of floss, strip the floss (separate out each individual strand and then lay them back together). This creates better sheen, especially in a satin stitch.
- Before using rayon thread, hold a working length by both ends and give it a quick snap. This helps relax the fibers and prevent tangling.
- Remove kinks from rayon threads by running them over a damp towel. Let dry before using.
- Knots are rarely used in embroidery. Instead, begin and end a thread by making several tiny stitches placed close together on the back where they won't show.
- Treat your hands to a non-greasy lotion, and then buff them on a dry towel. This prevents your hands from snagging in the fabric (especially silks).
- When threads start to tangle while you stitch, hold the work upside-down, letting the needle dangle so the thread can untwist.

Making Even Stitches

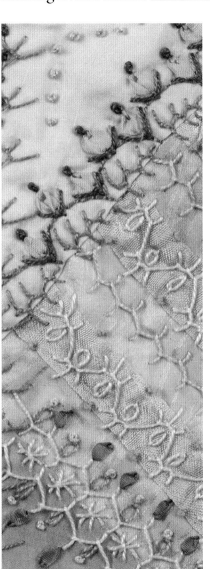

Making even stitches takes a lot of practice, so be patient with your stitching if you are a beginner. When learning a stitch for the first time, make lots of them on scrap fabric.

Also, practice making a stitch in very small to very large sizes—this will help you find a size that you are comfortable with. When you start embroidering your patched piece, work on different areas so "beginning" stitches will be less obvious. If you happen to put in stitches that you don't like, take them right out. It's perfectly okay to rip!

It isn't necessary to make totally even stitches. Creative interpretations are often more interesting to the eye. You can skew stitches at different angles, create a big stitch followed by a small stitch, or create a meandering line of stitches.

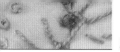

Stitch Combinations and Variations

There is an infinite number of ways to vary your stitches. Here are some ideas:

Layer stitches.

Stack stitches.

Thread or weave another fiber with stitches.

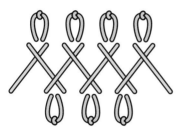

Add one stitch next to another.

Tie stitches (add tacking stitches).

Scatter stitches.

It's fine to work only one row of a stitch along a patch seam, especially when the interior of a patch is highly embellished. But try adding onto a base row and see what happens. Note how the character of the block changes as more stitches are added. Building up rows of embroidery creates visual interest and rhythm, blends one patch into another, and makes a more flowing composition overall.

Work a stitch onto each base row: Try the Fern Stitch in silk ribbon, Fly Stitch, ribbon stitches (silk ribbon), and threaded chenille.

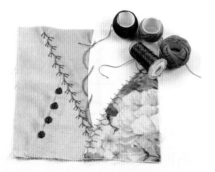

Work a base row along each patch edge. Here are Woven Roses, Double Feather, Outline, and Cretan Stitches.

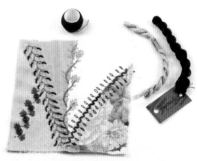

Finish up with French Knots, Bullion Stitch, and Lazy Daisy.

100 Embroidery Stitches

The stitches are grouped according to similarity in their construction or appearance. The Pekinese Stitch, for example, is grouped with Backstitch because it is a wrapped backstitch. The Cast-on Stitch is with Bullion Knot, because the results appear similar.

Some stitches are more difficult than others. Begin with the easy-looking stitches, and move on to the more complex ones as you feel ready. The photos will give you ideas for combining stitches, colors, and threads.

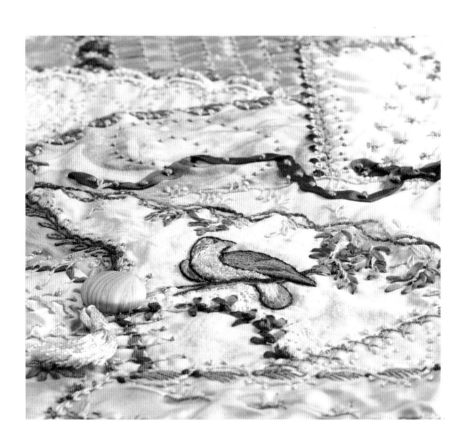

Backstitches

Backstitch

The reverse side of the Backstitch is the same as the Outline Stitch.

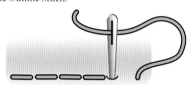

1 Bring the needle up a stitch length ahead of the previous stitch.

2 Go down using the same hole as the previous stitch.

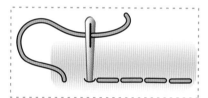

Left-handed version.

Split Stitch

Use this stitch to make neat outlines for embroideries.

Work the same as Backstitch, but stitch into each previous stitch, thus splitting the stitch.

Double-laced Backstitch

Work this stitch in one, two, or three colors

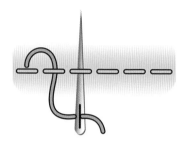

1 Work a row of Backstitch.

2 Fasten on a different thread and lace through the stitches without going through the fabric.

3 Work a second row in the other direction.

Chevron Stitch

The top and bottom bars of this stitch resemble small Backstitches. Work the stitch between two parallel imaginary lines, going from left to right.

base of the diagonal bar. Continue as in steps 2 and 3 at the top of the row, and then at the bottom.

1 Make a tiny stitch coming up halfway to where the thread comes through the fabric. This forms a short horizontal stitch at the top of the row.

2 Diagonally to the right, at the bottom of the row, make a tiny stitch.

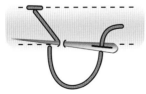

3 Stitch again to the right of the stitch made in step 2, coming up at the

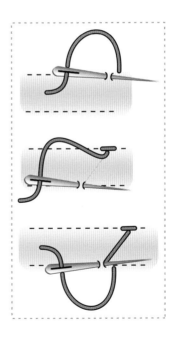

Left-handed version.

Pekinese Stitch

This decorative stitch is simply a laced Backstitch.

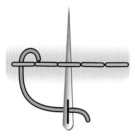

1 Work a row of Backstitch. Fasten on a second thread and pass the needle under the first stitch.

2 Skip a Backstitch, and bring the needle up under the following stitch. Pass the needle down through the skipped stitch, and repeat.

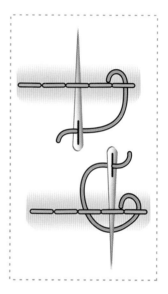

Left-handed version.

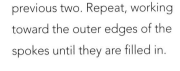

Raised Spider Web

Weave over each spoke, working clockwise without going through the fabric. The weaving is the same as the Backstitch.

previous two. Repeat, working toward the outer edges of the spokes until they are filled in.

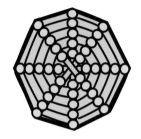

1 Use Straight Stitches to form any number of spokes.

2 Fasten on a second thread, and come up at the center of the spokes. Working clockwise, stitch over one spoke and under the

Blanket Stitch

Work this stitch toward either the right or the left. Vary it by making the vertical part of the stitch taller, shorter, closer together, or farther apart. You can also make some in the opposite direction (below the line).

1 Make a vertical stitch with the thread under the needle.

2 Make a second vertical stitch to the right of the first.

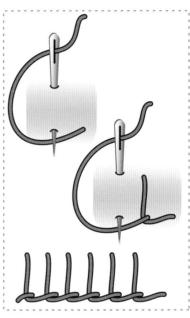

Left-handed version.

Buttonhole Stitch

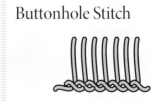

Work the same as the Blanket Stitch, but make the stitches exactly next to each other.

Blanket Stitch Fan

Work the Blanket Stitch using the same hole in the fabric to begin each stitch. Finish with a Straight Stitch to fill in the open area by the first stitch made.

2 Fasten on a second thread, and work lacing between the two rows without going through the fabric. When lacing, always keep the needle facing one direction only.

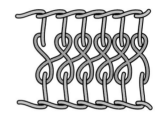

Laced Blanket Stitch

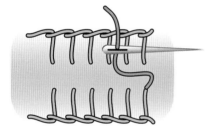

1 Work two rows of Blanket Stitch facing each other.

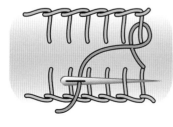

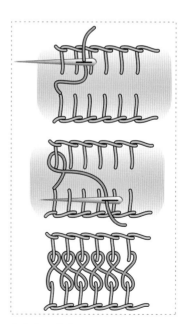

Left-handed version.

Closed or Crossed Blanket Stitch

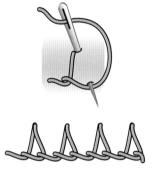

Make a Blanket Stitch, slanting the top. Work the next Blanket Stitch next to it, slanting the top to meet the first stitch. Continue to make the stitches in pairs.

Two vertical stitches meet at the top for the Closed Blanket. To make the Crossed Blanket, begin the second stitch to the left of the first.

Eyelet Stitch

This stitch is the Buttonhole stitch worked in a circular direction. Work either from right to left or left to right.

1 Draw a small circle inside a large circle on your fabric.

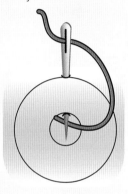

2 Bring the thread up anywhere along the center circle, and stitch from the outer circle to the inner one. Repeat.

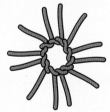

Detached Buttonhole Stitch

This stitch is dimensional—it sits above the fabric. Use Detached Buttonhole Stitches to create delicate-looking leaves for floral embroideries.

1 Make a Straight Stitch the length you want the finished stitch to be.

2 Work the Buttonhole Stitch onto it without going through the fabric. The stitches can be pulled tightly, or kept loose.

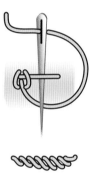

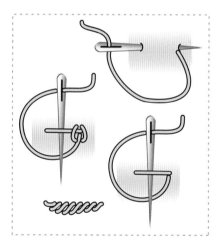

Left-handed version.

Knotted Buttonhole Stitch

A French knot forms at the top of each stitch.

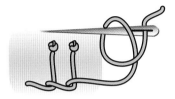

1 Wrap the thread over, then under the needle.

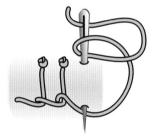

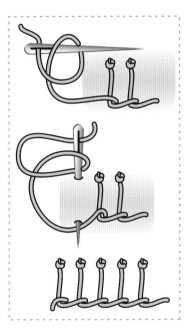

2 Insert the needle at the top of the row, coming up at the bottom. Pull the thread snug, and then pull the needle through the fabric.

Left-handed version.

Bullion Knot

Use a Milliner's needle for most threads, and use a Chenille needle for wools and silk ribbon.

1 Make a horizontal stitch the length you want the finished stitch to be; keep the needle in the fabric.

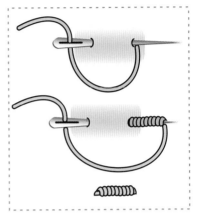

Left-handed version.

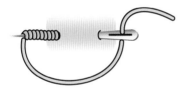

2 Wrap the thread evenly around the end of the needle to equal the distance of the stitch made in step 1.

3 Hold onto the wraps and gently coax the needle through. Sink the needle where the stitch began, and tug on the thread a little to settle the wraps in place.

Looped Bullion Knot

Make the Bullion Knot the same as above, but make the wrapped part of the stitch (step 2) twice as long as the first stitch made in step 1.

Cast-on Stitch

Make enough cast-on stitches to equal the desired size of the finished stitch. Use a Milliner's needle, and keep the stitches loose enough to slide off the needle.

1 Make a small stitch, but do not pull through.

2 Wrap the thread under and over your finger, and then pick it up onto the needle. Slide the stitch onto the needle so it forms a small knot.

Repeat to make a row of knots on the needle.

3 Pull the needle through the stitches, and sink the needle near the first stitch.

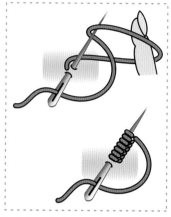

Left-handed version.

Bullion Knot Rose

These are wonderful in wool thread. Try them in silk ribbon also! The Bullion stitches can also be worked around a center of French Knots.

1 Stitch three short Bullion knots in a triangle, and then surround them with longer ones.

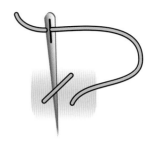

Palestrina Knot Stitch

This stitch is worked from left to right. Basically, it is a knot made on a bar of thread.

1 Stitch vertically, with the needle coming out at the bottom of the row.

2 Run the needle under the diagonal stitch made in step 1 without piercing the fabric.

3 Run the needle under the diagonal stitch a second time to the right of the first, having the thread under the tip of the needle.

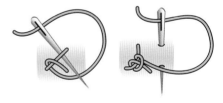

4 Pull through and tug on the stitch so the knot settles into place. Repeat steps 1–4 to make a row of knotted stitches.

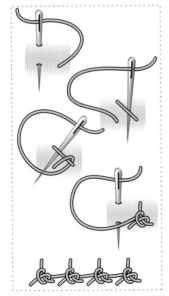

Left-handed version.

Chain Stitches

Chain Stitch

Make this stitch in any direction—left, right, up and down, or shaped to fit a curved line.

1 Place the needle in the fabric with the thread under the tip of the needle.

2 Pull through. Begin the following stitch next to where the thread came through from step 1. Continue.

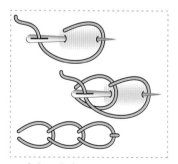

Left-handed version.

Cable Chain Stitch

This is a slight variation on the Chain Stitch.

1 Make one Chain Stitch.

2 Wrap the thread from the back to the front, and again to the back of the needle, and pull snug.

3 Place the needle into the fabric past the loop of the first chain, and make the stitch; have the thread under the tip of the needle. Repeat steps 2 and 3 to continue.

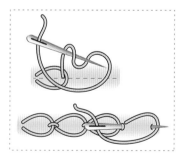

Left-handed version.

Magic Chain Stitch

For greater contrast, thread the needle with silk ribbon and a thread.

1 Thread the needle with two different colors of thread.

2 Work the Chain Stitch using one thread for the first stitch and the other for the second; continue.

3 End with two tacking stitches.

Open Chain Stitch

1 Make a Chain Stitch with the needle aimed diagonally.

2 Begin the next stitch at the dot. Repeat steps 1 and 2.

3 End with two tacking stitches.

Chain Stitch Rose

These roses are wonderful in silk ribbon! You can also try working the stitch around a cluster of French Knots.

Beginning at the center, work Chain Stitch in a circular fashion until the rose is the size desired. Start with small stitches at the center, and make them larger as you go.

Twisted Chain Stitch

1 Begin above the stitch with the needle aimed diagonally, bringing the needle up along the line of the stitch. Repeat.

2 End with a tacking stitch.

Coral Stitches

Coral Stitch

This stitch consists of small knots It is great for textured outlines.

Make a short diagonal stitch with the thread going over, then under the needle. Pull through, keeping the thread snug. Repeat.

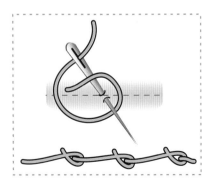

Left-handed version.

Knotted Coral Stitch

The Coral stitch worked as individual knots can be done in rows or scattered stitches.

1 Make a short vertical stitch through the fabric with the thread going over, then under the needle. Pull through, keeping the thread snug.

2 Sink the needle right next to the knot.

Knotted Cable Stitch

The knotted cable stitch is a fantastic combination of Coral, Lacing, and Chain Stitches.

1 Make a Coral Stitch and pull through.

3 Beginning slightly above the knotted and laced stitch just made, run the needle through the fabric with the thread under the tip of the needle—this forms a Chain Stitch. Repeat steps 1–3, and finish the row with a tacking stitch.

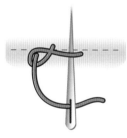

2 Pass the needle under the beginning of the stitch without piercing the fabric.

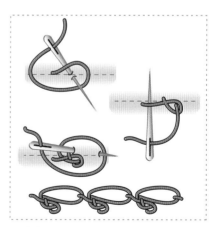

Left-handed version.

Long-armed Single Coral Stitch

Make these in a row. Work either to the left or the right.

1 Begin above an imaginary line and make a short vertical stitch with the thread going over, then under the needle. Pull through, keeping the thread snug.

2 Finish with a tacking stitch just beneath the knot made in step 1.

Knotted Herringbone Stitch

This fanciful stitch consists of the Zigzag Coral Stitch (see next page) worked onto a background row of Herringbone. Work from right to left.

1 Make a row of Herringbone Stitch. (See page 126.)

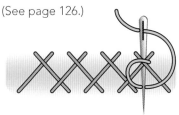

2 Fasten a second thread beside the upper "X" of the Herringbone.

3 Without piercing the fabric, run the needle behind the "X" with the thread under the tip of the needle. Pull through.

4 Place the needle behind the bottom "X" and run the needle through with the thread under the tip of the needle. Repeat steps 3 and 4.

Zigzag Coral Stitch

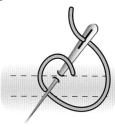

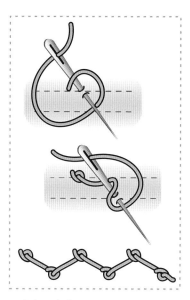

1 At the top of the row, make a short diagonal stitch with the thread going over and then under the needle. Pull through, keeping the thread snug.

Left-handed version.

2 Wrap the thread over the needle, then make a second Coral Stitch at the bottom of the row, wrapping the thread in the opposite direction.

3 Repeat steps 1 and 2.

Couching

Use couching to fasten down threads and fibers that are too thick to be sewn through the fabric. Finish the ends of the couched fiber by pulling them to the back with a large needle.

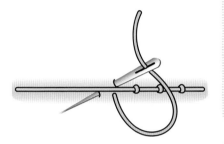

Fasten on a fiber to be couched by finishing its ends to the back. Fasten on a second thread, and stitch over the fiber at intervals.

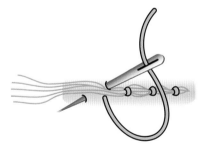

Couch multiple fibers by fastening one or both ends to the back. Make small stitches to hold the fibers in place.

Couching with Embroidery Stitches

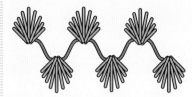

Fasten on a fiber to be couched, and work an embroidery stitch at intervals to hold it in place.

Thorn Stitch

Form Thorn Stitches in groups to represent foliage, or make them in rows along crazy patches.

1 Make a long Straight Stitch using a heavy thread.

2 With a second, finer thread, make pairs of short straight stitches that cross over the long stitch and hold it in place.

Filler Couching

Use filler couching to fill in embroideries or as a stand-alone stitch on a crazy patch.

1 Outline an area using the Outline or Split Stitch (see page 135).

2 Make long stitches vertically.

3 Make long stitches horizontally.

4 Couch the intersections of the long stitches.

Running Stitch

The multi-useful running stitch is used in quilting, sashiko, and for basting. The stitches are often made with equal lengths and spacing. Vary the stitch by making some shorter and closer together, and others longer or farther apart. Multiple rows of Running Stitches can be as decorative as any other stitch along a crazy patch edge. Try using metallic threads or silk ribbon for extra pizzazz.

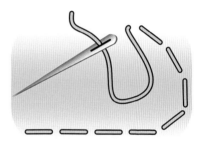

1 Make a line of evenly spaced stitches going through all layers of fabric. Running stitches can be done individually, or by taking several stitches onto the needle before pulling the needle through.

Overcast Running Stitch

1 Make a line of Running Stitches. Fasten on a second thread, and overcast by sliding the needle under each stitch; do not go through the fabric.

Holbein Stitch

Make a line of Running Stitches, spacing the stitches one stitch length apart. Fasten on a second thread at the end and make another row, filling in the leftover stitch spaces.

Interlaced Running Stitch

Interlacing and overcasting are very effective, especially with chenille, silk ribbon, or a variety of yarns.

Make a line of Running Stitches. Fasten on a second thread, and lace through the stitches without piercing the fabric. Turn back at the end or change to a different thread color, and lace in the opposite direction.

This antique silk quilt features a variety of embroidery stitches along patch edges. Detail. Museum Collection, Dyer Library/Saco Museum, Saco, Maine.

Cretan Stitch

To work this stitch, imagine three vertical lines.
Work downward.

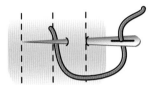

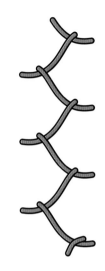

1 Make a stitch from right to left with the thread under the needle and not stitching all the way to the center line.

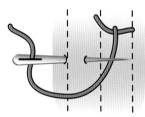

2 Pull through. Then, make the next stitch the same as in step 1, but from left to right. Repeat steps 1 and 2.

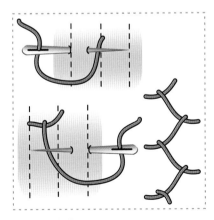

Left-handed version.

Knotted Cretan Stitch

This stitch is worked the same as the Cretan
Stitch, but with an added knot.

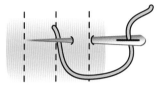

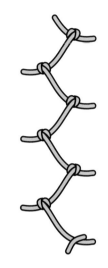

1 Make a stitch from right to left with
the thread under the needle; do
not stitch all the way to the center
line.

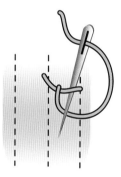

2 Pass the needle under the stitch
just made without piercing the
fabric, and pull snug.

3 Make the following stitch from left
to right, and knot the same as in
step 2. Repeat steps 1–3.

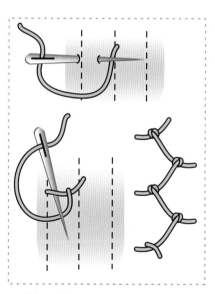

Left-handed version.

Raised Cretan Stitch

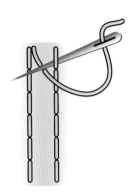

1 Work two rows of evenly spaced Backstitch (see page 73).

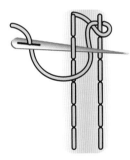

2 Work the Cretan Stitch onto the Backstitching without piercing the fabric.

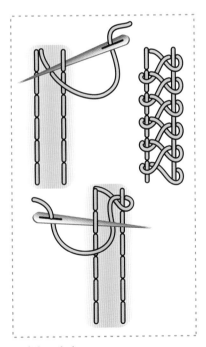

Left-handed version.

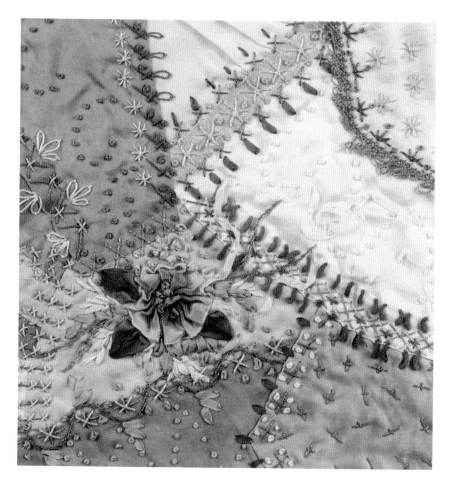

Cross Stitch

Often used on evenweave fabrics, Cross Stitch is also an attractive stitch for crazy quilting. Make cross stitches in neat rows, or scatter them unevenly on the fabric.

Make a stitch diagonally. Make a second stitch crossing the first.

Rice Stitch

This stitch is effective in two thread colors.

1 Make a row of large Cross Stitches.

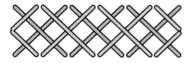

2 Make a second row crossing the first, but offsetting them.

Continuous Cross Stitch

Working Cross Stitches continuously creates an even row of stitches.

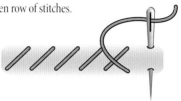

1 Stitching vertically, make a row of diagonal stitches.

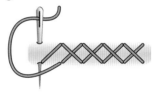

2 Go back over the first row with a second row of diagonal stitches.

Star Stitch

Scatter Star Stitches, make them in rows, or use them at the ends of Feather, Cretan, and other stitches. Vary the stitch by changing the size of the second Cross Stitch.

Make one Cross Stitch on top of another.

Moss Stitch

Invented by Marian Nichols, author of "Encyclo-
pedia of Embroidery Stitches," the Moss Stitch is
like a tied Cross Stitch.

1 Make a Cross Stitch; end by
bringing the needle up at the top
of the stitch.

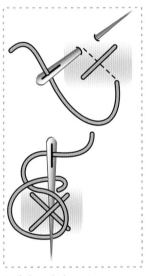

Left-handed version.

2 Form a loop, and place the needle
over the loop and through the
Cross Stitch without going through
the fabric. Pull through and sink the
needle below the stitch.

Victorian Fringe Stitch

Make fringe stitches close together or in multiple rows to make a thicker fringe. The fringes can be cut or left looped.

1 Thread the needle with a doubled thread.

2 Form the thread into a loop. This loop forms the fringe. Hold the loop in place, while making a short horizontal stitch. This begins a Cross Stitch.

3 Make an identical stitch below the first, forming half of the Cross Stitch.

4 Sink the needle at the top right corner, completing the Cross Stitch.

5 Begin the following stitch to the left of the first, bringing the needle up at the top of the Cross Stitch placement. Continue with step 2, sharing the holes of the first Cross Stitch.

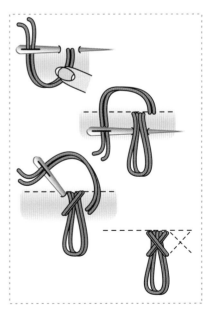

Left-handed version.

Feather Stitches

Feather Stitch

This stitch is a favorite for crazy quilting. Work it along patch edges, adding other stitches such as French Knots or Lazy Daisy to the ends, along the seams of pieced fans, and along the seams of a quilt after sewing the blocks together. Work downward.

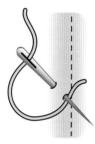

1 Stitch diagonally from left to right, stopping just short of an imaginary line in the center (see illustration). Pull through.

2 Make the next stitch diagonally from right to left on the opposite side of the line. Repeat steps 1 and 2.

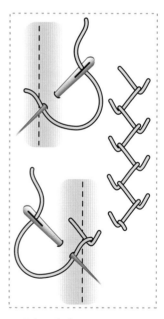

Left-handed version.

Chained Feather Stitch

This stitch consists of Lazy Daisy stitches (see page 130) worked in Feather stitch formation. Work downward.

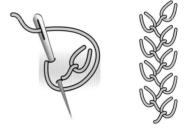

1 Stitch diagonally, keeping the thread under the needle. Pull through. This makes a Lazy Daisy stitch.

2 Insert the needle lower diagonally, and make a diagonal stitch the same length as the stitch made in step 1. Pull through.

3 Stitch diagonally, keeping the thread under the needle, to form a Lazy Daisy. Pull through. Repeat steps 1–3 beginning the following stitch beneath the Lazy Daisy made in step 1. End with a tacking stitch.

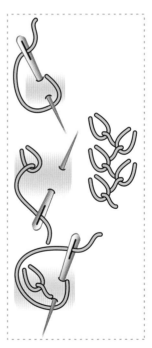

Left-handed version.

Double Feather Stitch

This stitch is formed the same way as the Feather Stitch, but with an extra "arm" at each side. Expand it further with three or more arms at each side. Work downward.

1 Complete the first step of the Feather Stitch.

2 Stitch diagonally from right to left on the opposite side of the line.

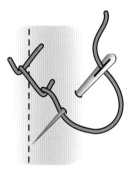

3 Make the next stitch to the right of the first. Make the following two stitches working toward the left, and repeat steps 2 and 3. End with a short tacking stitch.

Stacked Feather Stitch

Make the stitches very close together to form leaf shapes. Work downward.

Follow instructions for the Feather Stitch, but make the stitches closer together.

Straight-sided Feather Stitch

This stitch is the same as the Feather Stitch, but with straight "arms." Work downwards.

2 Make a short, vertical stitch to the right of the first and slightly lower. Repeat steps 1 and 2, working downward. The stitches should stack and look like columns.

1 Make a short, vertical stitch with the thread under the needle.

Fishbone Stitches

Fishbone Stitch

Fishbone Stitches make wonderful leaves, and they are especially nice with silk ribbon or ribbonwork. Begin by drawing a leaf shape with a center line on the fabric.

needle coming out slightly lower than the point of the leaf. Pull through.

1 Bring the needle up at the point of the leaf. Make a stitch from the center line diagonally upward to the right, with the needle coming out slightly lower than the starting point. Pull through. This makes a vertical stitch along the center of the leaf.

2 A little below the earlier stitch, stitch from slightly left of the center line diagonally upwards, with the

3 Stitch from slightly right of the center line diagonally upwards to just below the stitch made in step 2. Repeat steps 2 and 3. The stitches will overlap slightly at the center.

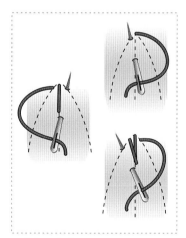

Left-handed version.

Open Fishbone Stitch

The center of the stitch forms an interesting zigzag pattern. Draw or follow three imaginary lines on the fabric.

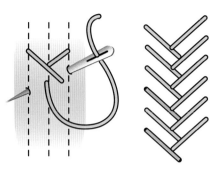

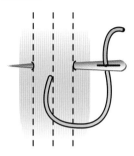

1 Come up at the center line and stitch horizontally just above the line, going from right side to left. Pull through.

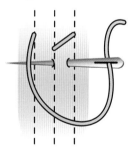

2 Make a short horizontal stitch (shorter than the distance from the center to the right side line) below the previous stitch, with the thread over the needle.

3 Stitch diagonally from right side to left—this stitch will match the very first stitch made. Repeat steps 2 and 3.

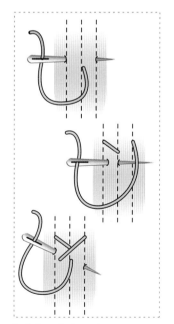

Left-handed version.

Fly Stitches

Fly Stitch

This stitch is very versatile and easy to do.

1 Stitch diagonally with the thread under the needle, so that the needle and the beginning thread form a "V" shape. Pull through.

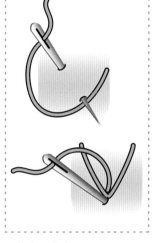

Left-handed version.

2 Make a small tacking stitch.

Crown Stitch

This is a variation on the Fly Stitch.

1 Make a wide and shallow Fly Stitch with a long tacking stitch.

2 Add two Straight Stitches.

Stacked Fly Stitch

1 Make a series of Fly Stitches vertically and close together.

Fly Stitch Variations

1 Begin the Fly Stitch, and then tack it using a Lazy Daisy (see page 130), French Knot (see page 120), Outline Stitch (see page 135), or Straight Stitch (see page 145).

Fern Stitch

Decorative by itself or use it for leaves.

1 Make a vertical stitch.

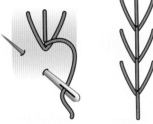

2 Make a Fly Stitch beneath the stitch made in step 1. Repeat step 2.

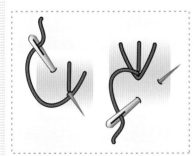

Left-handed version.

Tete de Boeuf

This is also called a "Wheatear Stitch."

1 Begin a wide and shallow Fly Stitch.

2 Tack with a Lazy Daisy stitch (see page 130).

French Knots

French Knot

Observe the direction of the wraps, otherwise the "knot" may slip through the fabric. Wrap the thread around the needle once, twice, or three times to vary the size of the knot.

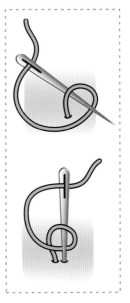

1 Wrap the thread over, then under the needle, pull snug.

Left-handed version.

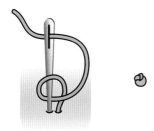

2 Sink the needle next to where the stitch begins (not in the same place).

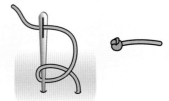

Continuous French Knot and Continuous Pistil Stitch

These stitches form a decorative line and are worked horizontally leftwards.

Place the stitches farther apart to make the Continuous Pistil stitch.

1 Wrap the thread over, then under the needle.

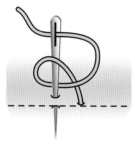

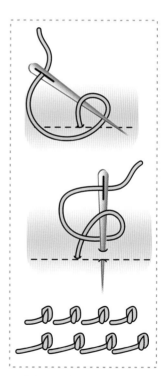

2 Make a short, vertical stitch. Pull the thread snug, and pull through. Repeat to make the following stitch to the left of the first.

Left-handed version.

Italian Knotted Border Stitch

This consists of long Fly Stitches tacked with French Knots.

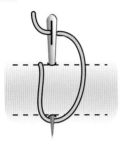

1 Make a long, narrow Fly Stitch (see page 116) and pull through.

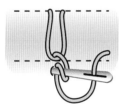

2 Make a French Knot to tack the Fly Stitch. Repeat to form a row, working in either direction.

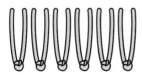

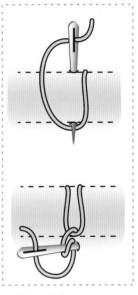

Left-handed version.

Four-legged Knot Stitch

A French Knot is formed at the center of a Cross stitch.

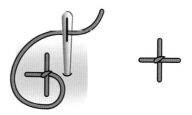

1 Make a vertical stitch to begin the Cross Stitch, and bring the needle up at the left side of the stitch. Pull through.

2 With the thread over the needle, slide the needle under the stitch made in step 1. Wrap the thread under the needle. Pull snug.

3 Pull through. The knot should be at the center of the Cross Stitch. Sink the needle at the right side of the stitch.

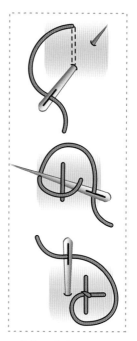

Left-handed version.

Colonial Knot

Often used in place of the French Knot, the two appear very similar.

one continuous action that feels like a figure 8 after you become familiar with the stitch.

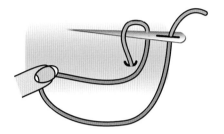

1 Scoop up the thread with the needle—note the direction of the thread in the diagram. If you are familiar with French Knots, this action is the opposite way.

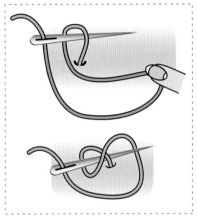

Left-handed version.

2 Bring the tip of the needle downward behind the thread and pick up the thread with the needle. Snug up the thread around the needle and sink the needle immediately next to where the stitch began. Steps 1 and 2 become

Herringbone Stitches

Herringbone Stitch

Work in a row toward the right. The needle always faces stitches that are already made.

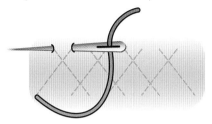

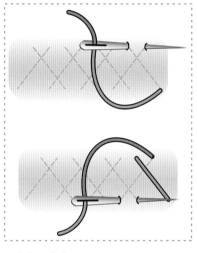

1 Make a small horizontal stitch at the top of the row, keeping the thread below the needle.

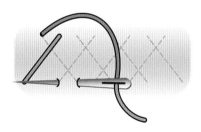

Left-handed version.

2 Make the following stitch at the bottom of the row, with the thread above the needle. Repeat steps 1 and 2.

Breton Stitch

This stitch is worked like the Herringbone, with an added wrap at the center.

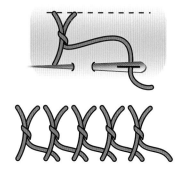

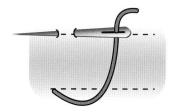

1 Make a small horizontal stitch at the top of the row, keeping the thread below the needle.

2 Without going through the fabric, bring the needle behind the beginning stitch. This creates a wrap around the stitch.

3 With the thread above the needle, stitch horizontally at the bottom of the row to the right of the stitch. Pull through. Repeat steps 1–3.

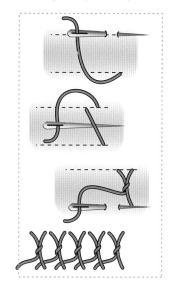

Left-handed version.

Closed Herringbone Stitch

There are two ways to work a closely spaced Herringbone stitch.

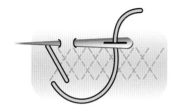

Make the same as the Herringbone, but place the stitches closely so that new stitches share the holes of the previous ones.

Another way to make the stitch is to first work a row of Herringbone stitch, and then go back over it with another offset row. This second row can be in a different color.

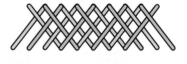

 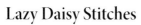

Lazy Daisy Stitch

Lazy Daisy is very simple, and it is often used to form flower petals. It is the singular version of the chain stitch. Do not pull the loop part of the stitch tight, or the rounded "petal" form will be lost.

1 Stitch vertically, and pull through.

2 End with a tacking stitch.

Twisted Lazy Daisy Stitch

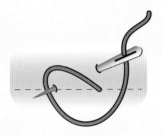

1 Begin by bringing the thread up along an imaginary line. Make a diagonal stitch from above the line and ending on the line. Keep the thread under the tip of the needle.

2 End with a tacking stitch.

Oyster Stitch

This stitch looks more complicated than it actually is. It begins with a Twisted Lazy Daisy that is then surrounded by a Lazy Daisy stitch. Make them in sync with the size of the thread (smaller with finer thread, larger with heavier thread) so they appear as textured "bumps" rather than defined Lazy Daisy stitches.

1 Working vertically, make a Twisted Lazy Daisy stitch.

2 Place your thumb on the thread beneath the stitch and run the needle under the upper right hand part of the stitch without piercing the fabric.

3 Pull through loosely, keeping your thumb in place.

4 Run the needle through the fabric from the top to the bottom of the stitch, keeping the looped thread at the bottom of the stitch under the needle. Bring the thread around the left side of the stitch and under the needle. Pull through, then make a short tacking stitch over both loops.

Lazy Daisy Variations

Vary the Lazy Daisy stitch by tacking it with a
French Knot (see page 120), Lazy Daisy (see page
130), Outline (see page 135), or Straight Stitch
(see page 145). You can also stack two stitches,
one inside the other.

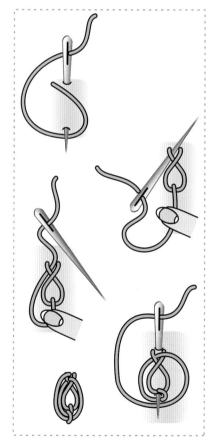

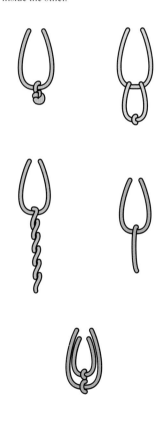

Left-handed version.

Basque Stitch

A fancy continuous version of the Lazy Daisy stitch with a twist. Work toward the right.

1 Make a vertical stitch, but do not pull through.

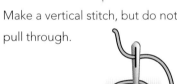

2 Wrap the thread in an "S" shape going behind, over, then under the needle. Pull through.

3 Working over the bottom of the loop just formed, Insert the needle

beneath the stitch, and come out at the top where the needle went in earlier. Pull through. Repeat steps 1–3.

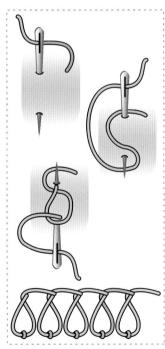

Left-handed version.

Outline Stitches

Outline Stitch

Stitch toward the right with the needle facing to the left. Make stitches immediately next to each other. This forms a neat, even Backstitch on the reverse. For a heavier line, overlap the stitches slightly.

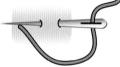

1 Make a small stitch with the needle facing previous stitching.

2 Repeat.

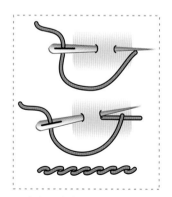

Left-handed version.

Overcast Outline Stitch

Overcasting can be worked from left to right, or right to left. Try overcasting using chenille, metallic, or other fancy threads or yarns.

Work a row of Outline Stitch. Fasten on a different thread. Working vertically, slide the needle under each stitch of the Outline Stitch without going through the fabric.

Outline Stitch Rose

Begin at the center and work Outline stitch in a circular fashion until the rose is the size desired. This can be worked around a cluster of French Knots.

Turkey Work

This stitch creates a "pile," which can either be looped or trimmed. Do not begin by fastening the thread to the fabric. Make all the stitches that go through the fabric as small as you can.

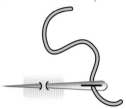

1 Make a tiny horizontal stitch.

2 Pull through and hold down the end of the thread with your thumb.

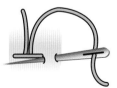

3 Make a tiny stitch to the right of the first, keeping the loop of the stitch for the pile.

4 Stitch to the right of the previous stitch with the thread under the needle. Repeat steps 3 and 4.

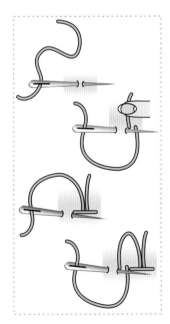

Left-handed version.

Satin Stitch

Often used for filling in motif embroideries, variations of Satin Stitch also have elegant charm and are useful stitches for the patch edges of a crazy quilt.

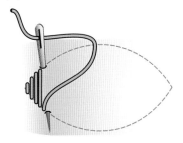

1 Stitch from one side to the other of the area to be filled in. For precise work, or with silk threads, bring the needle up at one side and pull through. Bring the needle down at the other side and pull through. Running the thread over a large needle or similar object while pulling through helps insure that the thread will lie smoothly.

2 For a thread-saving version of the stitch, bring the needle down at one side, and then up again at the same side with stitches very close together. This eliminates the stranding that otherwise occurs on the back.

Basket Satin Stitch

Make groups of Satin Stitches perpendicular to one other.

Woven Satin Stitch

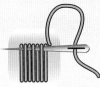

Work Satin Stitch in a small area. Fasten on a second thread, and weave back and forth until the area is filled in. You can sink the needle at the sides of the weaving, or weave the piece independently of the fabric.

Beetle Stitch

Work Satin Stitches into the same two holes in the fabric until the stitches mound up. Add details using French Knots (see page 120) and Straight Stitches (see page 145).

Laced Satin Stitch

1 Work Satin Stitches to create a row of blocks.

2 Fasten on a second thread, and without going through the fabric, lace between the blocks of Satin Stitch.

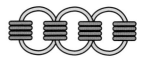

3 At the end, turn and go back the other way.

Padded Satin Stitch

This technique adds emphasis to the stitching. Use it for dimension, or to be sure an area is solidly covered.

1 Make a series of stitches going every which way within the design area.

2 Work Satin Stitches in one direction.

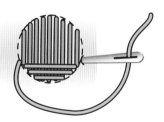

3 Work a second layer of Satin Stitch in the opposite direction.

Square and "V" Stitches

Square and "V" Stitches

Use the Straight Stitch to create various shapes, such as triangles, squares, and zigzags. This type of stitch is commonly and charmingly found on antique crazy quilts. These quilters may have had a limited repertoire of stitches and made them up instead.

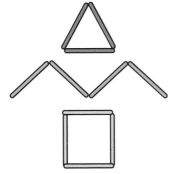

Form Straight Stitches to create shapes and patterns.

Add a tacking stitch to each section of Straight Stitch.

1 Stitch diagonally so the thread and the needle form a "V" shape. Pull through.

2 Tack with a small stitch.

3 Make a second stitch opposite, joining the ends.

Four-sided Stitch

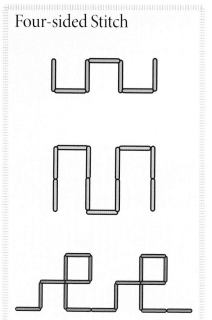

Use a Backstitch (see page 73) to form continuous rectangles and other shapes.

Arrow Stitch

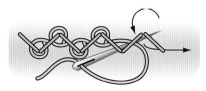

Make a row of "V" stitches using either Straight (see next page) or Fly Stitches (see page 116). Fasten on a second thread. Lace through the stitches, working in a circular fashion without going through the fabric. Follow the arrows.

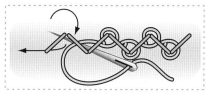

Left-handed version.

Straight Stitch

A Straight Stitch is simple as can be, and this stitch is also versatile and useful. Use it for flower stamens or petals, add fan-shaped groupings to other stitches, or scatter them along a patch edge.

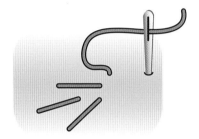

Go down through the fabric, making the stitch the length desired. Bring the needle up where you want the next stitch to begin, and repeat.

Seed Stitch

Place two small Straight Stitches side by side and repeat.

Straight Stitch Fan

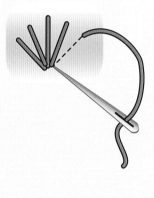

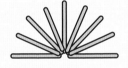

Make a fan shape, with stitches beginning at the top and converging at the base. Use as many stitches as needed, and shape the fan as desired.

Ermine Stitch

This is simply a Straight Stitch with a Cross Stitch on top. Scatter Ermine Stitches on the fabric, or make them in rows.

3 Sink the needle at the upper right side of the stitch.

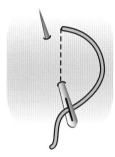

1 Make a Straight Stitch, bringing the needle up diagonally near the top of the stitch.

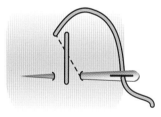

2 Stitch from the right to the left of the first stitch.

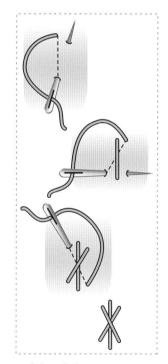

Left-handed version.

Sheaf Stitch

1 Make three vertical Straight stitches.

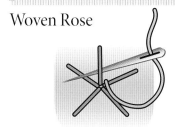

2 Pull the stitches together at the center with a tacking stitch.

Woven Rose

1 Make an odd number of spokes out of Straight Stitches, all converging at the center.

2 Fasten on a second thread, and weave around (over one and under the next) until the rose appears complete.

Algerian Eye Stitch

1 Make four Straight Stitches, each converging at the center.

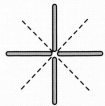

2 Make four diagonal stitches, converging at the center.

3 Add shorter stitches between each two of the previous ones all around, also converging at the center.

Wrapped Straight Stitch

1 Make a Straight stitch bringing the needle back up at the bottom.

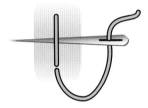

2 Pass the needle under the stitch without piercing the fabric.

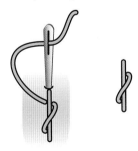

3 Sink the needle at the top of the stitch.

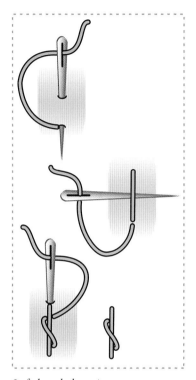

Left-handed version.

Tied Straight Stitch

Make a long Straight Stitch. Add one or more tacking stitches.

Embellishments

This Victorian crazy quilt is heavily embellished. Detail. Museum Collection, Dyer Library/Saco Museum, Saco, Maine.

Appliqué is sewing one piece of fabric onto another. This definition most often means sewing one piece of fabric onto another, but can be stretched to also mean sewing down an actual object such as a glove, or using other materials than fabric.

There are many types of fabrics that work well, especially plain cottons and rayon challis. For small shapes and maximum detail, use one of the finer weights of silk Habotai.

Work appliqué by hand or machine. Instructions for the hand method are below. For a machine method, follow the instructions given for Broderie Perse (see page 152).

Three appliqués are on this small block: a piece of leather cut into a glove shape, an iron-on transfer, and three small flowers cut from silk fabric. Note the strand of beads and the tiny button sewn to the leather glove. The flower stems are created from self-made cording (see page 161) couched down.

Materials:

Fabric scraps

Cotton sewing thread

Tools:

Size 12 Sharp needle, scissors, pins, sewing thread, and iron

Instructions:

1 Cut out the appliqué shape, adding a ⅛"–¼" seam allowance.

2 Press the edges under and pin to the fabric, or use the "needle-turn" method. For this method, do not pre-press, but use the sewing needle to tuck the edge before taking each stitch.

3 Invisibly hand-stitch in place using a slipstitch.

4 Embroider any details.

Pattern for Glove Appliqué. Cut out of lightweight leather, or use fabric and add seam allowances.

Slipstitch

Use this stitch for appliqué, or wherever you need to invisibly stitch a folded edge to another fabric. Fasten the thread to the back of the background fabric. Come up next to the appliqué. Slide the needle a very short ways along the inside of the creased edge of the appliqué, and then pick up a few threads of the background fabric. Pull through. Continue.

Broderie Perse/ Machine Appliqué

The Broderie Perse method uses an image from a piece of printed fabric. Apply by machine using the method here.

1 Cut out an image from printed fabric leaving an approximate ¼" seam allowance all around (no need to be exact).

2 By machine, straight stitch along the edge of the design, and along any lines that will be zigzagged.

3 Trim away the seam allowance as close as you can get to the stitching.

4 Set the machine for a short stitch and a width of zigzag that will cover the straight stitching and the cut edge. Sew along all previously stitched lines.

Beads

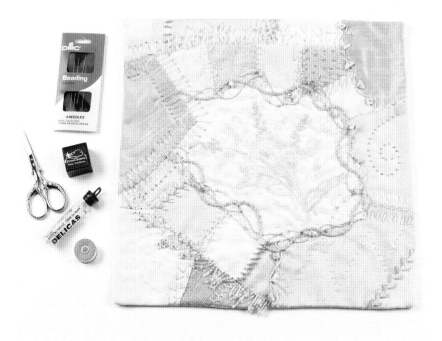

A tone-on-tone color scheme sets the mood for beading. Beads are sewn along lines of silk thread embroidery; they are also added randomly and in patterns on patch centers. Bead fringes and couched beads decorate patch edges. These particular beads include size 11 glass seed beads, bugles, and other assorted beads and semi-precious stones. Fabrics are suit-weight dupioni and other silks.

Add beads to highlight a row of embroidery stitches, or to replace the row entirely. Embellish motifs with them, or use beads to create motifs. Like other hard trims, they are not good for bed quilts. Save them for wall hangings, purses and other projects. A lot of glass beads can add considerable weight.

A wide selection of beads is available, and seed beads are best for embellishing quilts. I prefer size 11 beads, with other assorted sizes and bead types thrown in. Like buttons, collect whatever beads catch your eye.

Long needles made for beading are only necessary if you need to string on a quantity of beads at once. Otherwise, you can use any fine sewing needle that goes through the beads.

It's important to use thread made specifically for beading. Glass beads can cut through other types of threads. There are different weights of beading thread. Generally, the finer weights are for bead sewing methods in which the needle must go through a bead several times. A fine thread can always be doubled if it seems too thin.

Beading is easiest when you use a lap hoop (see page 64). Pour a few beads into a small dish and pick them up on the needle one by one.

To place several seed beads on the needle at once, place them into a small container and scoop the needle through the beads until you have as many as you need on the needle.

Materials:

Beads
Beading thread
Beeswax

Tools:

Fine sewing needle or beading needle and scissors

Instructions:

Thread a beading needle with a length of beading thread. Wax the thread and secure well to the back of the piece by making a series of tiny stitches close together. Be sure to anchor thread ends securely. Bring the thread up through the fabric.

There are two ways to fasten down a line of beads: backstitching and couching. (If you try to sew them individually, they may not space well.) Try both to see which works best for you.

With both methods, stop at regular intervals to make a few tiny stitches into the foundation fabric. This will prevent the beads from drooping, and will keep the beads from falling off if a thread happens to break.

Sewing on Individual Beads

The simplest way to sew on a bead is simply to sew through it and then down through the background fabric. Sew through the bead a second time for extra security.

Backstitching Beads

1 String on several beads (from two to six). Sew through the fabric at the end of the line of beads.

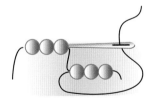

2 Bring the needle up at the center of the line of beads, and sew through the final beads. Repeat steps 1 and 2.

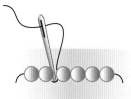

Couching Beads

1 Fasten on the beading thread. String as many beads as needed to make a row. Sew through the fabric at the end of the line of beads.

2 Going back the other way, bring the needle up at intervals and take tiny stitches over the bead thread.

Making a Bead Fringe

1 Fasten on the beading thread.

2 String on the number of beads needed for the length of the fringe.

3 Skip the last bead, and run the needle through the remaining beads and into the patch edge. At this point, make an extra tiny stitch to secure the fringe. Bring the needle to the next fringe placement and repeat.

Thick fringes are fun to make. Make a row of fringe, and then add additional rows until the fringe is as thick as you like.

You can use reproductions of vintage glass and metal, painted porcelain, crystal, dyed and plain shell buttons. The plain olive ones are antiques.

Really nice buttons are collectibles, and a crazy quilt is the perfect place to display them. Look for interesting buttons made of shell, ceramic, bone, wood, porcelain, mother of pearl, crystal, glass, metal, and other materials. You may also make silk-covered buttons.

Sew on buttons in clusters, or sew them individually to highlight patch seam embroidery. Use buttons to enhance motifs and silk ribbon embroideries. They tend to have a softening effect when attached singly or in small groupings at corners where patches come together. Sew them to your quilt with sewing thread, embroidery thread, silk ribbon, pearl cotton, or any fiber of your choice that can go through the buttonhole.

Covered Buttons

Use small scraps of hand-dyed or marbled silk fabrics to make covered buttons. Sew on a tassel (see page 164) along with the button, if you like.

Materials:

Inexpensive plastic buttons
Cotton batting
Silk fabric scraps
Thread

Tools:

Scissors and sewing needle

Instructions:

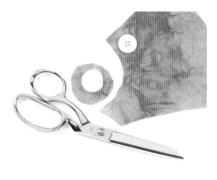

1 Cut a circle of batting the same size as the button.

2 Cut a circle of fabric twice the size of the button.

3 Thread a sewing needle, and sew a line of basting stitches at the outer edge of the fabric circle. With the fabric circle wrong-side up, place the batting circle in the center and the button on top. Pull the thread to gather, and stitch back and forth to hold the gathers in place. Fasten to your project by sewing invisibly around the edge.

Cigarette Silks

Vintage cigarette paraphernalia can be found in antiques venues. This photo shows both "silks" and felts. "Silks" are made from a silk satin surface placed over a core of some other fiber (possibly cotton). They were an advertising scheme, to be sent for after a quantity of cigarette packages were purchased. Prints included butterflies, ladies, flags, flowers, Queen Victoria's image, and other designs.

Felts are made from cotton flannel, sometimes larger than the silks. They were also printed with images, including rug designs, flags, and butterflies.

These antiques can be added to crazy quilts if they have not become too fragile. They should be handled carefully; tack them on with as few loosely made stitches as possible, using all-cotton thread. Placing these silks on a wall quilt is a way of both preserving and displaying them.

Cordings

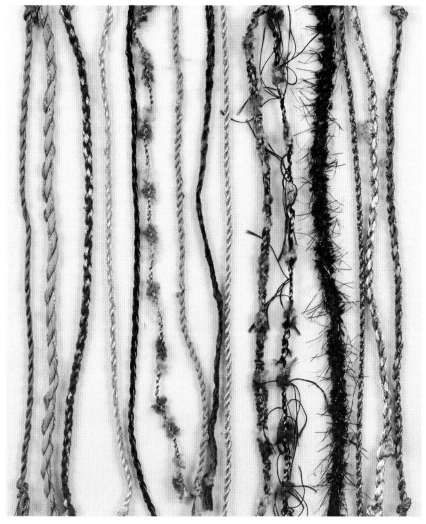

These fancy cordings are made of the same threads and fibers used to embroider crazy quilts: metallic threads, rayon and silk ribbons, fine textured yarns, rayon and cotton threads, and chenille.

With so many interesting fibers to choose from, you will never have to buy cording again. It is easy to make your own cordings, and they come in handy, so make a bagful to have on hand for projects. I pre-make them in the longest lengths possible, and then use from that piece until it is gone. Save cut offs by tying a knot at each end.

Couch or sew cording along the edges of crazy patches or on the centers of patches. Place cordings in straight or meandering lines; use them for flower stems or to outline a motif. Sew one to the outer edge of a miniature quilt. Use cording as a neckpiece for a pendant, hanging cord for a tassel (see page 164), or as a handle for a fabric purse.

Only one length of fiber is needed to make cording, but it's even more interesting to ply a bunch of different fibers. Experiment with your thread stash to find unique combinations. Use any sewing or embroidery thread, silk or rayon ribbon, metallic thread, or fine yarn. Hairy-looking yarns and other novelty yarns make interesting cordings. Silk ribbon comes out looking smooth and sleek.

To make cording, you will need an anchoring device, such as a hook. If you can, install a ½" cup hook at about waist height. If you cannot place a hook anywhere, use the presser foot of your sewing machine. You will need to be able to release the cording easily with one hand, so tying it onto something does not work.

A cord twisting tool makes the job go faster, or you can use a pencil instead. You will need a small weight so the cord will twist evenly. (Or, tie crochet string around a small rock and put an S hook on it).

Materials:

Threads and fibers of your choice

Tools:

Cord twister or pencil, and weight

Instructions:

1 Begin with a length of fibers a little longer than twice the desired finished length. Don't make it too long—you will need to be able to reach the middle.

2 Tie a knot at one end and place it onto a hook.

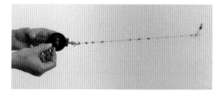

3 Tie a knot at the other end and place it onto the twister or pencil. Twist in one direction until the fiber starts to kink, and then turn the other way to take out some of the twist until the kinks go away.

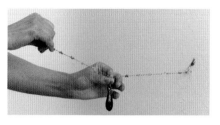

4 Take off the twister or pencil, and hold the cord out straight. Place the weight at the center of the cord. Hold the weight down to keep some tension on the cord, and bring the ends together.

5 Slide the other end off the hook. Hold the cord up in the air and let go of the weight. Let the cord twist until the weight stops turning. Finish by knotting the ends together.

As with self-made cording, making your own tassels means you can use the fibers of your choice. Use any threads, embroidery ribbons, or yarns. You can also combine several in one tassel.

Design the tassel—make it long and skinny, short and fat, or anywhere in between. Make contrasting wrappings and cordings. Tie beads into the tassel's fringe. Make the wrapped section out of threaded beads, or wrap with copper, brass, or silver wire. Sew tassels to your crazy quilt projects or quilts to accent a motif, embellish a button, or decorate a pieced fan.

Materials:

Small piece of cardboard

Threads or fine yarns of your choice

Tools:

Scissors and a sewing needle to fit the fiber

Instructions:

1 Make a length of cording (see page 161) twice as long as you want the hanging cord to be. (You can also use a heavy thread, such as pearl cotton.) Knot the ends together.

2 Cut a piece of cardboard the length you want the tassel to be. Wind the thread or yarn around the cardboard as shown.

3 Cut through the fibers and lay them out flat. Place the hanging cord on the fibers with its knot just below the center. Thread the needle with about 24" of the same fiber, and run this under the cut lengths. At the end of the thread, tie a knot that brings the cut fibers together just above the knot of the hanging cord. Cut the tying thread and set the threaded needle aside.

4 Fold the cut fibers downward to cover the knot of the hanging cord. With the threaded needle, make wraps placing them about ½" or so below the top of the tassel. Sew back and forth through the wrapped section a few times, and then run the needle down through the tassel. Trim all ends even.

This patched and basted block includes one gathered, one tucked, one scrunched, and one pintucked patch. The scrunched patch is "tacked" with sewn-on beads. The block is ready for embroidery and more embellishment.

Often, creating dimension on a crazy quilt results from embellishing on top of flat patches. But why not begin a dimensional quilt by giving three-dimensional shape to the patches themselves? Treating patch fabrics to pintucks, pleats, tucks, or gathering is easy to do, and placing some of these on a foundation creates an interesting quilt top.

Besides breaking up the monotony of flat patching, dimensional patches are also fun to embellish. Be creative! Use embroidery stitches, silk ribbon embroidery, beads, and buttons to hold pleats, gathers, and scrunches in place.

Pintucks

Make pintucked fabric as one large piece, using a quarter or a half yard of fabric, and then cut the sewn piece into patch-sized pieces as needed. A sewing machine makes this go quicker, but you can also make pintucks by sewing fine hand stitches.

1 Fold or press creases into the fabric. Place them randomly, or use a ruler and mark equal intervals with pins. Machine sew less than ⅛" from the creased edges.

2 This step is optional. Fold the fabric and sew a pintuck perpendicular to the first stitching. This turns the folds of the first stitching in the direction of the sewing. Fold the fabric for the next row of stitching, and sew either in the opposite or in the same direction as the first, depending on which way you want

Gathering

Begin with a piece of fabric a few inches larger than needed for a patch.

1 Set the sewing machine to do a long stitch, or thread a hand sewing needle with matching thread, and sew across the patch.

2 Pull up on one of the threads to gather the fabric. Bring the threads to the back and tie the thread ends at both ends.

Scrunching

1 Lay a patch that is too big for its space. "Tame" the excess with small stitches, beads, or other embellishments.

Tucks and Pleats

There are two ways to prepare tucked and pleated fabrics. You can do one patch at a time, cutting each patch large enough to accommodate the take-up, or you can press or stitch folds into fabric and cut patches of it. Begin with a quarter or a half-yard piece of fabric.

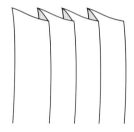

1 Press a series of folds into the fabric.

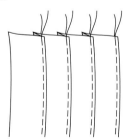

2 Machine or hand sew along the creases, or leave them loose.

Fans are beautiful on crazy quilts, and there are many ways to use them. Make pieced fans to fit into the corners of a quilt's border, or use an individual fan as a patch on a crazy quilt.

Sew accurate fans by piecing them directly onto a paper pattern. The paper piecing method makes it easy to sew perfect fans, even using fine silk fabrics.

There are many ways to design fans. The standard fan shape in the instructions is a quarter of a circle. Experiment by sketching fan shapes that are wider or narrower than this. Lengthen and increase the number of blades. Shape the ends of the blades rounded so the fan itself is scalloped. Add a handle.

After a fan is pieced (steps 1–3 on the following pages), place it onto foundation fabric. Finish the rounded edge by pressing it under ¼" or so. Or, cover the raw edges with a wide ribbon or trim. The outer edges of the blades will be sewn into seams if the fan is used in a corner. If using as a patch, lay other patches to cover the raw edges.

Materials:

Tracing paper or photocopies (see Instructions)
Fabrics
Sewing thread

Tools:

Scissors, pencil, ruler, sewing machine, and pins

Make a Paper Pattern:

1 To make a quarter circle fan pattern, draw a large circle onto a sheet of paper (trace around a plate).

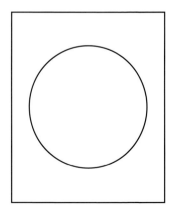

2 Cut out the circle and fold it into quarters.

3 Cut out one of the quarters. Mark the fan center using a ruler to make it an even distance from the point.

4 Fold the paper evenly to indicate six or more fan blades. Mark the blades with pencil and ruler. Fasten the fan to a larger sheet of paper and trace around it. Use this to make the copies needed (see sew the fan).

Sew the Fan:

1 Draw a fan to the size needed. Make a copy or tracing for each fan that you are making. Make a separate copy or tracing for each fan center. Pre-cut fabric pieces for the blades about an inch larger on all sides than the pattern blades.

2 Stack the first two blades right sides together, and place behind the first blade of the drawing. Stitch along the line, then trim the seam allowance even. Open out the second blade and press. Continue to add one blade at a time until all are sewn on.

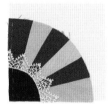

3 Cut a piece of fabric for the fan center, being sure to add seam allowances. Press the upper edge to the back. Slipstitch the fan center to the blades. Remove the paper from the back of the fan before it is placed on the foundation, and baste the fan in place.

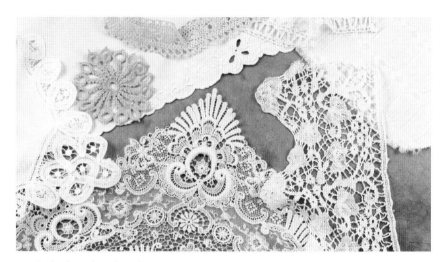

Quality laces show their elegance no matter how they are placed on a crazy quilt, so seeking out good lace is well worth it. Shops selling bridal, heirloom sewing, or couture supplies will have a selection.

There are different kinds of laces. Tape laces, such as Battenberg, consist of narrow "tapes" formed into designs that are held in place with threads woven into fanciful designs. Woven, knitted, or crocheted laces are flat or gathered, and often made of cotton. Venices are intricate and dimensional laces or motifs, made of rayon or cotton, and often used for bridal wear.

You can buy laces new, used, or well aged. Used clothing stores and yard sales are great places to find bridal and evening wear that can

be scavenged for their details (like buttons, laces, and patch fabrics), and some antiques venders specialize in textiles. Vintage lace often has twice the charm of new laces. Do not cut up whole pieces of lace; if they are intact, they should remain that way. Whole doilies are very nice on crazy quilts, especially when tacked to a large central patch. Smaller doilies can adorn corner blocks. Damaged laces are very useful, since you can trim them to fit anywhere.

Insert laces into patch seams as the block or quilt top is patched, and place them across patches or along seams.

You can also make your own special laces. Common lace-making methods include knitting, crochet, tatting, bobbin lace, and Battenberg.

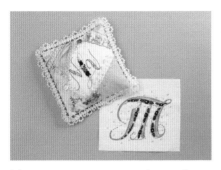

Materials:

Paper

Tracing paper

Embroidery materials

Tools:

Pencil, ruler, and embroidery tools

There are many ways to outline and fill in the letters of monograms with embroidery. The "M" is outlined in couched metal braid. Both monograms feature silk ribbon embroidery.

An extraordinary monogram is more than a signature; it can be a highlight of a quilt.

Draw your initials, and transfer them to a patch on a crazy quilt top or block. Embroider along the lines using Outline, Split Stitch, French Knots, or Couching. The letters can be widened out and filled in with Satin Stitch, French Knots, or silk ribbon embroidery. Make a fancy monogram by overlapping the letters. You can even write out your whole name, transfer it, and embroider.

On another patch, embroider the date you finished the quilt.

Instructions:

1 Begin with sketched letters or letters enlarged on a computer's word processor and printed out.

2 Use tracing paper to adapt and arrange the letters as you want them. You may want to try several arrangements then choose the one that appeals to you. Use a ruler if needed to line up the letters.

3 Transfer the monogram to fabric using the Tracing Paper Transfer Method (see page 176).

Beautiful floral embroideries were the highlight of many a vintage crazy quilt. Detail. Museum Collection, Dyer Library/Saco Museum, Saco, Maine.

Small motif embroideries both warm up and personalize a crazy quilt. Choose images that you enjoy, or create motifs to follow the theme of the quilt, if it has one. Sketch your ideas, then use the Tracing Paper Transfer Method (see page 176) to place an image onto a crazy patch or fabric.

Use the stitches of your choosing to fill in a motif. Satin Stitch is commonly used for fill-in embroidery. Other stitches can be used as well; try using closely worked rows of Outline Stitch, tightly packed French Knots, Chenille couched to fill an area, and so on. Flosses are the thread of choice for filling in motifs. See Threads on page 65. See also Embroidery Tips on page 68.

Conversely, there is no need to fill in motif embroideries. Embroideries simply worked as outlines are also attractive (and often found on antique crazy quilts). Use Outline Stitch, Backstitch, or Split Stitch.

Work embroideries on individual fabrics to use as crazy patches, or work them directly onto a patched quilt top.

Tracing Paper Transfer Method

This is an easy and foolproof way to transfer the outlines of an embroidery design onto fabric. This method leaves no marks or residue.

Materials:

Artist's tracing paper
Embroidery materials
Basting thread

Tools:

Hard-lead pencil, paper scissors, embroidery hoop (quilter's lap hoop preferred), and sewing needle

Instructions:

1 Position your work in a quilter's lap hoop. This will keep the tracing paper flat, and you will have both hands free to work the embroidery.

2 With a hard-lead pencil, trace the design onto the tracing paper.

3 Cut out the design, leaving about ½" of paper around it.

4 Place the tracing on the patch or fabric to be embroidered, and baste all around the paper.

5 Embroider the outlines of the design, and then tear away the paper. Finish the embroidery.

Tree trunk embroidered in outline stitch, with leaves worked in punchneedle.
Variegated silk flosses from the Caron Collection.

Punchneedle goes quickly and results in a carpet-like pile. You can do an entire design in punchneedle, or parts of it using embroidery for the rest.

Punch needles come in a range of sizes, from very fine to large needles. The finest needles take one strand of silk floss. This is the best size for filling in small and detailed motifs. The larger needles work with heavier threads or yarns and are good for other types of projects.

To transfer a design, use the Tracing Paper Transfer method on page 176. To work punch-needle, begin on the right side of the work and embroider the outline of the design using Outline Stitch or Backstitch. This makes a neat edge on the front of the work while providing a guideline on the back.

Begin punching along the outlines, and then fill in areas. Your fill-in may seem scanty at first, and that's normal. Keep working over an area until the density of the punching makes it difficult to punch. (But be careful to not break the needle.) You will have a nice, thick carpet-like pile on the front of your piece.

To shade and blend colors for realistic effects, use no more than a yard of floss at a time. Because you will need to re-thread anyway, it is easy to change to a different shade. Work over the area until it is filled with the different colors. Using variegated threads is another way achieve blended effects.

Once you are finished punching, you will have a loop nap, which can be sheared if you want it fuzzy. If the nap is uneven, the higher loops can be sheared, keeping others as loops. You may find that silk thread colors deepen an entire shade after shearing, so try a small area first to see if this is desirable.

Materials:

Silk embroidery floss or other fine thread

Tools:

Punch needle in a small size to fit one strand of silk floss, threader, small embroidery hoop, and embroidery scissors

Tips for Success:

- Use two layers of fabric. Work punchneedle after a quilt top or block is patched so there is an extra layer of the foundation. This helps "grab" the stitches and hold them in place.

- Stretch the fabric tightly in an embroidery hoop. Use a small (4"–6") hand-held hoop. To keep the fabric taut, use the fingers of the hand holding the hoop to push up from underneath near the punched area.

- Keep checking to make sure the thread is free to travel. Threads can easily catch on things or become tangled.

- Keep the open side of the punchneedle facing outward, and use a punch-slide motion, staying in contact with the fabric. The punchneedle should be held upright or at a bit of a slant.

Instructions:

1 Transfer and outline a design on the right side of the fabric as described above. Reverse the fabric in the hoop so the wrong side is facing up.

2 Thread the punchneedle. Follow instructions for threading that came with the needle. If there are no instructions, use the threader to bring the thread down the shaft and through the needle end. Remove the threader, and then insert it through the eye of the needle to bring the thread from the inside (the hollow side) to the outside of the needle.

3 Begin with about an inch of thread coming through the eye of the needle. Punch the design, filling it in and shading as desired.

4 Trim thread ends close to the fabric.

The antiqued look of this motif was accomplished by lightly brushing small amounts of metallic acrylic paints onto the flowers, leaves and the crocheted doily. Four different types of ribbon are used: 7 mm silk, ½"-wide graduated rayon, 1"-wide velvet, and 1"-wide bias-cut.

There are many ways to shape and work with ribbons. Fasten them down flat and embroider along them; sew them into flower and leaf shapes; ruche them into squiggled, ruffled trims; or make bow ties and streamers.

Collect many types of ribbons and experiment. Some ribbons are flat woven, making them ideal for tight gathering, thick flowers, and accordion roses. Satin ribbons are thicker than flat-woven ones, and silk ribbons are luxurious. Buy white silk, satin or plain woven ribbons, and dye them to have as many colors as you like. Rayon ribbons that are graduated (shaded from side to side) are especially nice for flowers and leaves. Grosgrain ribbons have a nice texture, and narrow ribbons can be sewn in meandering lines on patches or tied into bows.

Some ribbons have wired edges, and these are good for shaping flower petals. Wires don't gather the ribbon as well as thread, so you might want to remove the wire if you need a gathered edge. Use general-purpose scissors for cutting wired ribbons.

Like ribbons, laces with finished edges may be used to make the trims and florals on the following pages.

Ribbon Trims

Make gathered ribbon trims, and baste them along the edges of patches or across patches. Fasten them on with embroidery stitches, beads, or silk ribbon embroidery along the edges or along the gathers.

Begin with a ribbon that is 1½–2 times longer than the finished length. The basting in each of the following instructions is assumed to be "by hand" because flowers and trims are shaped and sewn by hand.

Materials:

Ribbons
100% cotton sewing thread

Tools:

Sewing needle and scissors

Instructions:

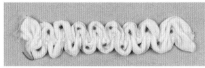

1 Fasten a sewing thread to one end of a ribbon and sew a line of basting along the center. Pull up on the thread to gather. Fasten off.

2 Fasten a sewing thread to the upper edge of a ribbon, and sew a line of basting. Thread a second needle, and baste along the lower edge. Pull up on both threads together to gather the ribbon. Fasten off each thread.

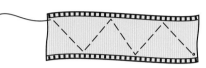

3 Fasten a sewing thread to one end of a ribbon and sew a line of basting in a zigzag fashion. Pull up on the thread to gather. Fasten off.

Winding Flower

1 Fasten a sewing thread to one end of ribbon that is about 16" long, and sew a line of basting along the edge. Pull up on the thread to gather the ribbon. Fasten off.

2 Sew or pin one end of the ribbon to a crazy patch. Wind the free end around. Sew the flower in place, concealing the ribbon end.

Gathered Flowers

Premake flowers in this section in quantity, and then place and pin them onto your project. Sew them in place while shaping the edges at the same time. Different lengths of ribbon will give different results. For a flower, begin with about 8", and also try longer and shorter lengths. For berries and buds, use about 3"–4" of ribbon. Make Prairie Point leaves (see page 185), and sew them on along with the flowers.

Circle Flower

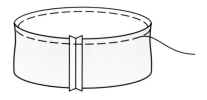

Sew together the ends of a length of ribbon. Sew a line of basting along one edge. Pull up on the thread tightly. Fasten off.

Double Flower

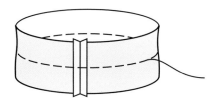

Sew together the ends of a length of ribbon. Sew a line of basting along the center. Pull up on the thread tightly. Fasten off.

A gathered flower with "petals" of narrow ribbons knotted and stitched at the flower's center.

Berries and Buds

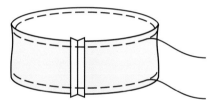

Sew together the ends of a short length of ribbon. Sew a line of basting along each edge. Pull up on both threads tightly. Fasten off.

Folded Flowers and Leaf

Folding ribbons is another way to form ribbon flowers, and a simple way to make a leaf.

Accordion Rose

Make a bunch of these and sew them onto a quilt top in clusters. Begin with about 9"–12" of soft ribbon (silk or rayon) ⅜"–¾" wide. Thread a needle with matching thread and set aside.

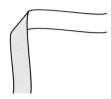

1 Begin at the center of the ribbon and fold the left end downward.

2 Fold the same end upwards toward the back.

3 Fold the right end to the back. Continue to fold, always folding toward the back and alternating the ends. Hold the final folds and let go of the previous ones. Take one of the ends and pull downwards slowly. As soon as the rose forms, stop pulling. Stitch through the base then down through the center of the rose to hold it in shape. Trim off the ends of the ribbon.

Prairie Point Leaf

Make a pile of these; you may want to have two or three for each flower that you make. They are especially nice in graduated ribbon. The finished size of the leaf depends on the width of the ribbon. Use ribbon ¾"–2" wide. Ribbon narrower than ¾" makes extremely tiny leaves that are difficult to handle.

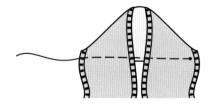

Fold both ends of the ribbon downward. Baste across, making sure the basting includes all layers of the ribbon. Pull up to gather. Fasten off. Trim the ends of the ribbon.

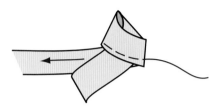

Tea Rose or Rosebud

This works best in a wide ribbon. Keep the folds loose as you form the bud or tea rose. The folds should be exaggeratedly large to make a rose. Use about 14" of 1½" wide ribbon. Thread a needle with matching thread and set it aside.

2 Take the long end of the ribbon and fold it loosely to the back. Sew through the base, gathering the layers. Continue folding the ribbon loosely around the base, and stitch as needed to gather and hold the layers together.

3 Trim the ribbon ends close to the stitching. When sewing the rose or bud to a crazy patch, fold the lowest petal down to conceal the stitching.

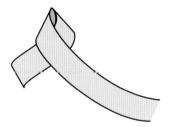

1 Begin toward one end of the ribbon and fold both ends downward, following the diagram.

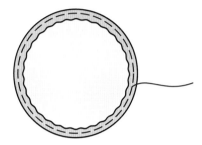

Fabric Flowers

Yo-yos and large dramatic flowers (see next page) are made of fabric, not ribbon, but are similar enough to ribbon flowers that they are included here. Use lightweight silk fabrics, or other lightweight fabrics. The Large Flower can be made of very wide ribbons, especially hand-dyed bias-cut silk ones. Add silk ribbon embroidery details to yo-yos to complete the look of a flower.

Yo-Yos

Cut a circle of fabric twice the size of the finished yo-yo.

1 Fold or press the outer edge in, and baste around the folded edge.

2 Pull up tightly on the basting thread to gather. The raw edges of the circle will be inside the yo-yo. Fasten off.

3 Flatten out the yo-yo, centering the gathered opening. Invisibly stitch the yo-yo to the background fabric.

This vintage-looking flower is made out of a gauzy metallic fabric.

Large Dramatic Flower

If you need a large focal point, this is the flower. Use 2½"-wide lightweight ribbon or fabric. Make four or more petals for each flower. Add stamens, if you like, as you sew the flower together.

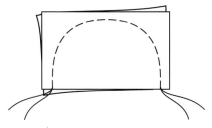

1 Cut two pieces of fabric or ribbon each 2½" by 3". Place them right sides together, and machine or hand sew a petal shape as shown in the diagram. Trim the seam evenly, clip the curves, turn, and press. Repeat to make the number of petals needed.

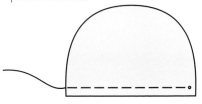

2 To assemble the petals, sew a line of basting along the lower edge of each and pull up to gather. Fasten off. Sew the petals to each other at the gathered bases.

3 Sew the center of the flower to background fabric and tack around the edges of the petals, shaping the petals as desired. Make a gathered flower (see page 183) out of ½"-wide ribbon and sew to the center.

Silk Ribbon Embroidery

Silk ribbon embroidery seems to belong on crazy quilts. It's a quick way to add a touch of luxury and some dimensionality. No other technique mimics flowers so well, especially if they are embroidered in variegated or shaded ribbons. To make lots of colors, buy a large spool of white silk ribbon and dye lengths of it (see Dyes for Silks on page 195).

A simple technique lets the ribbon settle smoothly onto the fabric so that flowers and leaves can be formed free of twists. Place your work in a lap hoop to have both hands free. As you sew a stitch with one hand, hold a large needle in the other and run the ribbon over it, removing the needle as the stitch is completed.

Use silk ribbons that are made for embroidery. Other types may be used, but are usually more difficult to work with, and results will not be the same. The quality of silk ribbon varies. Some are more loosely woven and they do not hold up to stitching very well. I prefer ribbons that are made in Japan—brand names vary since these are often repackaged.

The most common embroidery ribbon width is 4 mm. For finer stitches or small details, use 2 mm. For larger, more flamboyant stitches, use 7 mm.

There are a few stitches that are especially for ribbon—see the following pages. Other embroidery stitches that are especially good for silk ribbon florals include:

- Fly Stitch: Use for buds and flowers.
- Lazy Daisy: Use for flower buds and rose leaves.
- Feather Stitch: Use for branches and ferns.
- Fern Stitch
- Woven Rose
- Outline Stitch Rose
- Star (crossed stitches) Stitch: Use for flower centers or small flowers.
- Bullion Stitch: Use for buds or leaves.

Materials:

Silk ribbons for embroidery

Tools:

Size 18 Chenille needle, embroidery hoop, and embroidery scissors

1 Thread the needle: Run the ribbon through the eye, and stab the same end with the point of the needle.

2 Pull on the long end of the ribbon, and the "knot" will settle into the needle's eye.

3 To fasten onto the back of the fabric, make a tiny stitch and run the needle through the tail of the stitch to the front of the fabric.

Ribbon Stitch

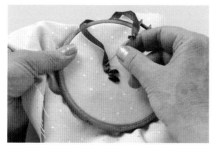

Flatten the ribbon onto the surface of the fabric and stitch through it. Stop pulling when the leaf shape is formed. Great for leaves and petals!

Pierced Loop Stitch

Begin the same as for the Ribbon Stitch, but make a short stitch. Pull through leaving a loop. Make the following stitch carefully to avoid pulling on the loop.

Twisted Straight Stitch

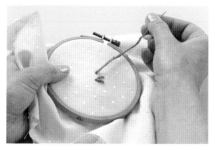

Twist the ribbon before making the stitch. Great for leaves and flower petals. This twisting technique can be used with other stitches as well, including Fly, Feather, and Fern Stitches.

Sloppy French Knot

Although these can also be done in thread, they are exceptional in silk ribbon. Use them for making small flowers and to fill in around an embroidery. Make a French Knot the usual way, but keep the ribbon very loose around the needle. Make two, three, or more wraps to vary the stitch.

This example shows 7 mm-wide silk ribbons used as the warp (dark red), and both 4 mm and 7 mm as the weft. Ribbons made from other fabrics may also be used.

Weaving your own patches avoids patching monotony—they will add interesting detail to a quilt top. Make one or more of these on your foundation fabric before adding adjoining patches. After weaving, add surrounding patches so they lap onto and conceal the ribbon ends.

Work some embroidery on the weaving so it is held in place firmly. Consider adding French Knots or beads to some of the intersections, or use a random embroidery, such as a silk ribbon floral.

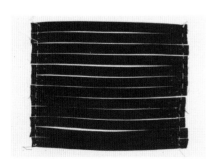

1 Lay ribbons evenly to form the warp and pin the ends. Baste along the pins and remove them.

2 Weave ribbons through for the weft, and pin the ends. Baste, removing the pins.

Spiders and Webs

Spider webs are particularly effective on dark fabrics. Use either gold or silver metal thread for the web.

Spider webs are common on antique crazy quilts. Create a web by couching (see page 221) metallic threads. Make a spider using embroidery stitches such as bullion, straight, and French Knots, or use a combination of stitches and beads. (Spiders have eight legs.)

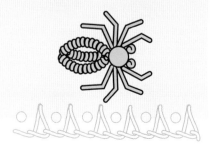

Surface Work

The frog patch on this antique crazy quilt is a painting. Detail. Museum Collection, Dyer Library/Saco Museum, Saco, Maine.

Surface techniques are methods that integrate color into or onto the surface of the fabric. Try some or all of these and you will never be bored by your fabrics again. These are great ways to stretch your supply of patching fabrics—buy one yard of silk for instance, and dye, paint, stamp, or stencil your way to a myriad of patches—each one new and different. Many of the methods can be combined. For example, create a stamped background and stencil onto it.

Dyeing silk fabrics is amazingly simple to do. You can dye as you go, creating the colors you want as you need them. Dye anything made of silk, including fabrics, ribbons, and threads.

Dyeing is economical. After learning how to dye my own, it was suddenly affordable to make a crazy quilt out of silks. Buy one-yard lengths of three or four different types of silk fabrics, cut each length into smaller pieces, and dye yourself a wide assortment of colors.

Instant-setting dyes work quickly and require no after-treatment. They come in concentrated form, so adding water is essential. If you use a container of dye multiple times, the fabric will come out paler each time. You can keep using a container of dye until all the dye is gone from it.

Dyed fabrics appear darker when wet and a lot lighter when dry, so if you are trying for a particular shade, mix the color darker and dry the fabric to see how it turned out.

Wear rubber gloves if you will be sticking your fingers into the dye, and consult "The Magic of Crazy Quilting" for mixing instructions to create a full range of colors.

Materials:

Set of instant-setting silk dyes (see Sources)
Distilled water
Silk

Tools:

8 or more eye droppers, tongs or tweezers, sheet of plastic, rubber gloves, and small plastic cups

Instructions:

1 Cover your work surface with plastic. Prewash the fabrics and roll them in a towel to soak up excess moisture. Cut the damp fabrics into pieces that are patch-sized or larger.

want the piece dyed evenly. For a mottled effect, crumple it up and set it in, and after a few minutes turn it over and leave it for a few minutes more.

2 Place about ½ cup of water in a plastic container. Using one eyedropper for each bottle of dye, mix the desired color. How many drops you add depends on how dark you want the color to be. Repeat for the number of colors you want.

3 Place a piece of fabric into the dye and stir for a few minutes if you

4 Remove the fabric with tongs or tweezers, let drip, and then set aside.

5 Individually wash the fabrics with mild soap and cool running water. Roll them in a towel, hang to dry, and press. Wash the containers, eyedroppers, and tweezers, and save them for the next dyeing.

Painting Fabric

Use acrylic paint to create motifs, enhance laces and trims, change the color of a motif, or create a background for embroidery. There are a variety of acrylic paints that you can buy, including standard opaque, translucent, metallic (gold, silver, bronze, copper), and pearlescent types. Some of these paints are great for highlights—you can even bronze a piece of lace!

Only prepare the colors that you will need right away. Acrylic paints dry quickly and once dry, they cannot be reliquified. Give a paint plenty of time to completely dry before using or heat setting.

For instructions for painting motifs and other small pictures, refer to books that show how to achieve different effects, use brushes, mix paints, and so on. To paint small pictures, stretch the fabric in a hoop so it stays stable while you paint.

Materials:
Acrylic paints
Water
Fabric

Tools:
Brushes in varying sizes, container for water, artist's palette, embroidery hoop, and a sheet of plastic to protect the work surface

The silk, velvet ribbons, and laces were painted prior to assembly for a wonderful antique look. The paints are metallic and pearlescent acrylics.

Create small paintings on pieces of silk or other fabrics; then use them as appliques or patches for a crazy quilt. Motifs and laces are often available in only white or off-white, but you can easily paint them. Pretreat motifs, ribbons, and laces by dabbing some paint on them. Let dry, and then heat set.

Heat-Setting Paints

Your painted fabric will be washable once the paints are heat set. This is simple to do and requires only a dry iron and press cloth. Protect your ironing board with the press cloth. Lay the fabric painting right-side down on the press cloth. Press with the iron at the highest heat the fabric will take for about 30 seconds. Repeat over the entire painting.

Marbling

Materials:

3 colors of acrylic paint

Carrageenan (see Sources)

Alum

Dispersing agent (see Sources)

Fabric

Tools:

Quart jar, disposable aluminum baking pan, 3 small containers, 3 eyedroppers, tools for swirling the paint, and a sheet of plastic to protect the work surface

Some preparation is involved in setting up for creating marbled fabrics, but the dramatic results are well worth it.

Preparation is important. You will need to get started a day before you do the marbling. Work on a kitchen counter next to a sink. Experiment with different tools for swirling the paint. I prefer a chopstick, but combs and other objects work well, too.

The acrylic paint must be very fine in texture. Paints that are designated for airbrush use are preferred.

Instructions:

1 A day ahead of time, mix one tablespoon of carrageenan into a quart of very hot water, and shake or stir vigorously until dissolved. Let cool, then refrigerate for 24 hours. This allows the mixture to gel and lets air bubbles rise to the top.

2 Take the carrageenan out of the refrigerator, pour it into the baking pan and let it warm to room temperature.

3 Prewash the fabric. Dissolve ⅛ cup of alum in a quart of hot water, and let it cool to room temperature. Dip the fabric in and take it out immediately. (The fabric will rot if the alum is hot, or if it is kept in the alum for too long.) Allow the fabric to dry, and cut it into pieces that will fit in the pan.

4 Place paint into each of the small containers. Mix water into each until the paint has the consistency of whole milk. Add a drop of dispersing agent to each color.

5 Using the eyedroppers, place drops of paint onto the carrageenan in the pan. The paint should spread out a little, and most of it should stay on the surface. If it all sinks, try thinning the paint. If that doesn't work, re-mix the carrageenan solution using a little more carrageenan.

6 With a comb, chopstick, or other tool, draw the paint into swirls. Place a piece of fabric on top and leave it for five seconds. Lift it off carefully, then rinse immediately under cool running water. Place the fabric aside on a flat surface.

7 To continue, either remove the paint from the surface of the carrageenan with strips of torn newspaper, or simply add more drops of paint and swirl.

8 Let the marbled fabrics air dry, and then heat set the paint.

Stamping

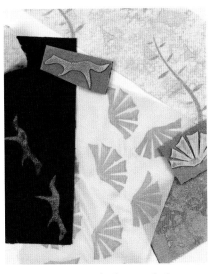

There are lots of opportunities for stamping, since it is so easy. Stamping is merely dabbing an object into paint and then stamping it onto fabric. You can cut out shapes from potatoes or other carvable objects to make small images, or you can use a sponge to create a textured look.

An easy way to make a stamp is to cut shapes out of leather and glue them to a cardboard backing. Use a very sharp, small scissors to get fine detail. A padded surface works best for transferring the paint to fabric. Use an old towel or folded fabric.

Experiment on scrap fabrics before using your good ones. Different types of paints (translucent, opaque, metallic, and pearlescent) will show up differently, and colors will react in varying ways to different backgrounds. Smooth and coarse fabrics will look different when stamped.

The stamped samples here include: sponge stamping, sponge stamping with an overlaid stenciled design, and stampings made from leather cut-outs.

Materials:

Acrylic paints
Paintbrushes
Fabric

Tools:

Objects for stamps, plate or flat surface for paint, paintbrushes, old towel, and a sheet of plastic to protect the work surface

Instructions:

1 Lay the towel on the work surface, with the fabric on top. Mix the paint colors as desired on the plate, spreading the paint with a brush.

2 Dip the stamping object into the paint, and then press onto the fabric. If this does not produce a good image, try applying the paint to the object using a brush before stamping.

3 Allow the paint to dry completely, and then heat set.

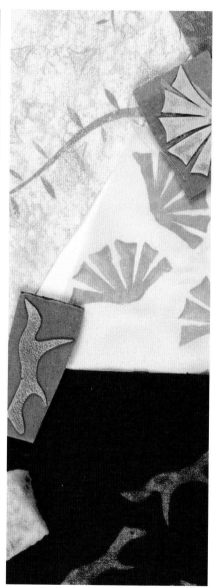

Stencils

Some interesting fabric backgrounds can be created by stenciling. You can buy stencils, but it is easy to make your own. Cut out shapes from plain white computer paper, and use them as temporary stencils. If you need a sturdier paper, use freezer paper, stenciling with the plastic side facing down.

Stenciled designs combine well with embroidery, or stand alone as distinctive patternings on fabric. The ribbons are stencilled, then foiled (see page 208).

Try to keep the image areas small, or you will be using a lot of paint. I find that plain computer paper works fine for several images. Let it dry, then turn it over and stencil from the other side. This strengthens the paper and reverses the design if it is not symmetrical.

Experiment with folding paper and cutting out snowflakes. Fold paper in half and create symmetrical designs, or carefully cut out a design such as the tree shown here. Make sure to cut your stencils with enough paper left around the outer edge so you can hold it in place easily, and so you won't be stamping off the edge of it.

Try a range of fabrics—many smooth cloths work well. Stenciled designs practically glow on cotton velveteen.

You will need a special brush shaped round with a flat end. These come in a range of sizes, the one I use the most is about ¾" in diameter. The brush is used vertically with a stamping motion. If you want, fasten the stencil down with a bit of masking tape. I simply hold the paper stencil in place while stamping; for small designs, this works fine.

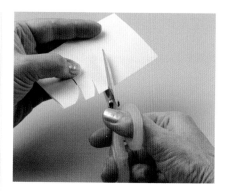

Fold paper into fourths or in half, and cut out the design areas.

Materials:

Acrylic paints

Plain white computer paper

Fabric

Tools:

Plate, paint brush, stencil brush, paper scissors, and a sheet of plastic to protect the work surface

Instructions:

1 Spread the paint out on the plate using a plain paint brush. If it is runny, it is probably too wet. Spread it thin so it dries out a little.

2 Dab the brush into the paint—use just a little bit of paint—and then stamp the brush on a piece of scrap paper or fabric. You should see a small amount of color transferred (but not gobs of paint). The paint should go on with a "dry" feel. Stamp a few more times if the paint is too thick.

3 Place your stencil on the fabric, hold it steady and begin stamping. The paint builds up slowly, don't try to lay it all on at once. Gradually build up enough paint to fill in all of the image areas. Remove the stencil as soon as you are finished, and let the fabric dry.

4 Heat set.

This is not a project for ordinary crayons. Use a paint or pastel stick that is made with dye. Be sure to follow any instructions that came with your dye sticks.

Take rubbings from any object that will make an interesting design on fabric, such as laces, textured fabric such as burlap, leaves, ferns, and gravestones. Make sure the dye does not come through the fabric to damage any items you may be using. If this happens, protect the item with a very thin sheet of plastic.

Experiment using different types of fabrics. Some will work well and show a good image; others will not. I prefer thin, smooth silks. They work beautifully. Be sure to stretch silks in an embroidery hoop so they do not shift.

Simple paper stencils (see page 203) also work for rubbings, or you can cut shapes out of poster board.

Rubbings result in soft-looking images. Four different rubbing samples make up this block. Images are taken from a piece of burlap, an all-over lace, a paper stencil, and a poster board cut out.

Materials:
Dye crayons
Masking tape
Fabrics

Tools:
Any interesting surfaces to take rubbings from, sheet of plastic to protect the work surface, dry iron, and an embroidery hoop, if needed

Instructions:

1 Tack the paper stencil or poster board design to another sheet of paper, using a drop of glue so it stays in place. Secure the fabric over the object using masking tape. Or, place the fabric in an embroidery hoop, stretching it tautly (necessary for thin silks).

2 Lightly rub the dye crayon over the surface of the fabric until the design comes through. Continue until it is as dark as you want it to be.

3 Cover your ironing board with a protective cloth.

4 Place the rubbing between two sheets of plain paper and iron. As the papers take up the wax from the dye crayon, change to clean sheets of paper and iron again. Repeat until the wax is removed.

The secret to foiling is adhesive. There are two foiling techniques: one requires an iron to stick the foil to the adhesive. Another uses only adhesive and no iron. The instructions below are for the iron-on method. Omit the iron if your materials do not require it.

The one drawback of foiling is its fragility in cleaning. You cannot machine-dry or dry clean a foiled design, or it will lose or dull the foil. It also will require press-cloth protection in ironing.

Tip:

After foiling, the adhesive is easily cleaned up using cool water.

Images are best on smooth fabrics; edges get blurred on napped fabrics.

Apply the adhesive in the design of your choice using any of the following methods.

If you want to add some flash to your crazy quilting, try foil. It will certainly add drama! Use foil to make individual images, or to highlight other techniques. The yellow piece includes stampings (see below). The ribbons are finished with iron-on metallic trims.

Stamping

My favorite found objects are shapes I've made in wire. Use 18- or 20-gauge wire made for jewelry wire working, bend a shape and hammer it flat. Also raid your kitchen for shapes such as the tines of a fork. Place adhesive onto the object by dipping or by painting it on, then stamp the fabric. Reapply adhesive for each stamping if doing more than one.

Stencils

Use stencils as per the instructions given for stenciling, using adhesive instead of paint. Paper stencils will hold up for fewer uses than with paint.

Paintbrush

Paint the adhesive directly onto fabric using artist's paint brushes.

Materials:

Foil
Foil transfer adhesive, (both specially made for foiling—see Sources)
Fabrics

Tools:

Dry iron, brush or foam applicator, and found objects

Instructions:

1 Apply the adhesive onto fabric evenly and thinly in your chosen design, using any of the methods described above.

2 Allow the glue to dry completely— this could take a few hours.

3 Place the foil with color side up over the adhesive on the fabric.

4 Use a dry iron. Heat the iron to a cotton setting (medium-hot) and rub (burnish) with the edge of the iron until the foil is transferred. You will be able to see the design on the surface of the foil. (If the foil melts, the iron is too hot.) Let everything cool, and then peel the foil sheet off. Repeat if the foil does not "take." Some foil colors may work better than others.

Photo Transfer and Inkjet Printing

Placing images on crazy patches makes inviting motifs. Transfer photos, or copyright-free images, and then appliqué them onto a crazy quilt. Then, embellish and embroider around them.

There are two ways to do this. You can photocopy, or iron a heat-transfer onto fabric. Or, you can use an inkjet printer to print from your computer directly onto fabric.

The following is general information only. Results will vary, depending on the products, equipment, method, and fabric. As with anything else, be willing to experiment. Be sure to follow any instructions that come with products that you use.

With either method, leave some area around the image for seam allowance.

Antique greeting cards offer out-of-copyright images that are wonderful on crazy quilts. The images here were photocopied onto transfer paper, then ironed onto silk satin fabric to be used as appliqués.

Photocopy

Take your photo or other image to a photocopying service that has a full-color laser photocopier. Have it photocopied onto heat transfer paper. If your image is one-directional (text), make sure it is copied in reverse so it will be the right way when you iron it onto fabric. It is a good idea to make several small test images, too. Use these to make sure your fabric choice will work (and if they turn out well, you will have the extra images for quilt décor).

Next, iron the image onto fabric. A smooth cotton is usually the fabric of choice. However, I prefer to use silk satin, which allows details to show up better. Choose a fabric that will take the heat of the iron. A flat solid surface, such as a cutting board, is usually recommended instead of an ironing board, but an ironing board works fine for small images.

Instructions:

1 Trim away any excess paper from your image.

2 Heat a dry iron to its highest setting.

3 Iron the fabric to heat it up, then lay the transfer in place.

4 Apply pressure for about 20 seconds to fasten the transfer down, and then iron for about 3 minutes.

5 While everything is still hot, carefully and evenly peel off the backing paper.

Inkjet Printer

First, make sure that your color inkjet printer has a permanent ink.

Use digital or scanned photos, scanned images, photos on CDs, text from a word processor, or art you make in a drawing or painting program—in other words, anything that can be generated on the computer and outputted to the printer. Be careful to check for copyright infringement before printing your images.

Fabric requires pretreatment; otherwise, colors may fade after printing, or ink colors may bleed. A number of manufacturers make pretreated and paper-backed fabrics. Products may vary, so be sure to follow the manufacturer's instructions. Various pretreated cotton and silk fabrics are available.

Do a test run with paper to see how the image will come out. Use the printer settings for maximum ink, and select options to allow the printer to feed a thicker sheet. The printed fabric may require washing to remove excess dye.

The finished images should be colorfast and hand washable.

Machine Methods

Surface decoration using a sewing machine expands your repertoire of embroidery and embellishment opportunities.

The value of machine work on a crazy quilt is its difference from hand work. The staccato of perfectly even, small stitches is an entirely different effect from hand embroidery. Machine work tends to flatten out surfaces it is applied to, while hand work does not. To acknowledge these differences is a way of understanding that the two do not replace each other, and each brings to a quilt top a much different appearance. The two can work well side by side, and they can be used to enhance each other. Use hand embroidery to enhance machine work, and add machine methods to hand work.

Sewing Machine

Any basic sewing machine can be used. It should do straight stitching and zigzag. The best preparation for creative machine work is to read the manual that came with the machine. It will tell you everything the machine is designed to do, give instructions for correct settings, which needles to use for which purposes, and more. The following machine methods are ideas and suggestions and should be considered an addition to your manual. Most techniques work best if you sew slowly.

Machine Needles

Have a collection of machine needles in several sizes including embroidery, denim, metallic, quilting and others. Match the needle to the thread or the task. Heavier fabrics and thicker threads require larger needles. If a needle breaks too easily, try a heavier one.

Stabilizers

With machine methods the base fabric may have a tendency to rumple as you sew. Use a stabilizer to get pucker-free results. Experiment with the many types available to find what works for you. These come in tissue-like paper, wash-away, tear-away, and other types. Often, artist's tracing paper, or computer paper work just as well. Place the stabilizer on the back of your work while sewing, and carefully remove it when afterwards.

Transferring Designs

The Tracing Paper Transfer method on page 176 works equally well for machine work. No hoop is needed because the tissue acts as a stabilizer. Pin the tracing in place and machine sew along the lines of the design. When finished, tear away the paper.

Tying Off Ends

Keep your machine stitching looking neat by finishing all thread ends to the back. To clean finish the ends leave a few inches of thread hanging on both back and front.

1 On the back of the work, use a seam ripper to pull up on the final stitch.

2 Pull on both the loop and the thread end and bring the top thread through to the back.

3 Tie both ends in a square knot.

Layering is an important concept when considering machine embellishment. Since machine work is basically flat (non-dimensional), keep-the-eye-moving interest is created by overlapping or building up layers. Note how the embroideries converge on each other creating an overall texture or composition for the whole piece rather than individual elements. The eye is free to travel.

The fabrics in this pillow top are mostly cottons. The machine sewing was done with YLI Variegated quilting, YLI Fine Metallic, DMC size 12 Pearl, and DMC Flower threads. Hand work is in YLI silk ribbon, DMC size 8 pearl cotton, and YLI Pearl Crown Rayon thread.

This is the nine-block Monet's Garden Floor Pillow featured on the cover of *Crazy Quilts by Machine*. After six years of using it, I took it apart at the seams, ripped off a lot of the hand work and kept the machine embroidery. (Yes, it's ok to go back and redo your stuff.)

The new pillow has:

- Machine embroideries of dragonflies, leaves and stems of plants, spider webs
- Machine straight stitching along patch edges
- Couched self-made cordings, couched variety yarns
- Insets
- Machine quilting in patterns
- Trapunto
- Silk ribbon sewn by machine

Touches of hand embroidery with threads and silk ribbon complete the design providing dimension and details. Hard trims, like beads, were not used.

Creating Fabrics

Here are some ways to make use of small pieces of fabrics and even your tiniest scraps to create larger, patch-sized pieces. Personally, I find silks too precious to trash, so I accumulate tiny fabric scraps and thread ends in a basket, and later find ways to use them.

The created fabrics shown here include strips of fabrics, ribbons and trims pieced together; small fabric scraps pieced; and organza sandwich.

To make fabric:

• Piece together strips of two or more different fabrics.

• Sew small fabric scraps together.

• Using a very narrow seam allowance, sew together ribbons, trims, or laces.

Make an organza sandwich:

• Choose any sturdy backing fabric such as a smooth cotton or silk. Onto this, layer snippets of fabrics, ribbons, and threads. Over the top lay silk organza fabric either plain or dyed in the color of your choice. Thread the machine with the thread of your choice and machine sew over the piece until it is all held together. Use stabilizer underneath if needed.

organza ⟶
snippets ⟶
backing fabric ⟶
stabilizer ⟶

Organza sandwich

Straight Stitch

The plain, straight stitch of a sewing machine is perfect for decorating patch edges. Although regular sewing or quilting thread will work, a heavier thread has more "punch" on a quilt top. Experiment to find threads that will work with your machine. Use a large, denim needle. Size 12 pearl cotton should work, and size 8 may also. The pearl cottons are easy to use because they are on a spool. If you want to try other types of embroidery threads, keep an empty spool handy to wrap the thread onto.

Adjust the stitch length to 4 mm or even longer if the machine allows.

Sew slowly. If you are sewing in a pattern (see the illustration), you may want to count the stitches between turns to keep the stitching even. It's fun to sew spiral or swirly designs on the centers of patches.

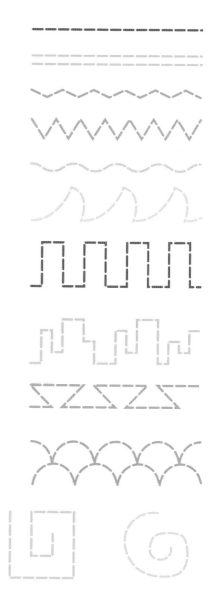

Couching

Couching consists of sewing a fiber onto a surface. It is done by hand (see page 96) or machine. By machine, a zigzag stitch fastens the fiber in place. Couch fibers along patch edges, or couch them into designs within patches.

Thread the machine with regular cotton sewing thread, or silk, rayon, clear nylon, or any thread that will work with zigzag stitching. The thread can match or contrast with the fiber being couched.

Set the machine's zigzag to a width that plunks down on either side of the couched material. Your machine may have a special foot with a hole through which a couching fiber can be threaded. The size of the hole may limit your fiber choices. Often, a regular foot or an embroidery foot works well.

The length of the stitch depends on the effect you want. A shorter stitch will show more thread, and a longer one will show more couching fiber.

Combine couching with self-made cording (see page 161), and make some interesting cords to couch onto your project.

Zigzag Satin Stitching

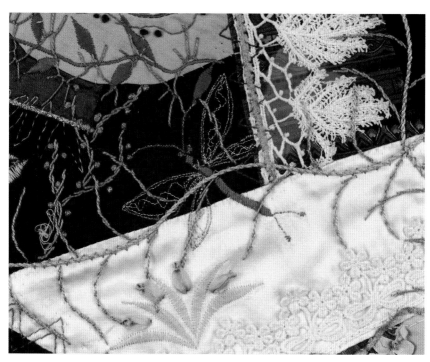

Zigzag satin is great for creating leaves to which you can add silk ribbon embroidered flowers (see page 180), and for designs such as the dragonfly in the photo. The technique is done by changing the width of the zigzag while sewing.

Thread the machine with a size 50 cotton or silk thread, or size 40 rayon thread. Use a matching cotton thread in the bobbin.

Shorten the stitch length so the sewing just barely goes forwards.

Place a stabilizer underneath. Run the machine at a slow speed, and operate the zigzag control from zero to its widest point, and back to zero again. Watch a leaf shape form. Form a narrow line with the zigzag set just above zero. This makes a stem. Continue in the designs of your choice.

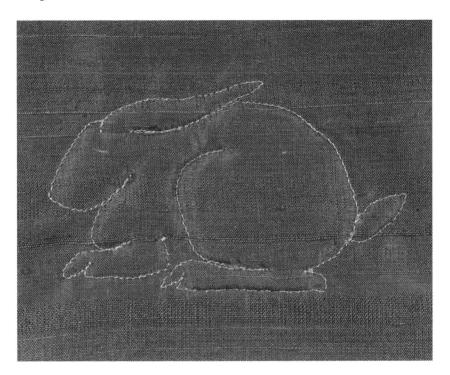

Trapunto consists of sewing an enclosed area, and placing padding inside. Because it requires two layers, it is ideal for working onto crazy patches that are sewn onto a foundation.

Begin by tracing or drawing an outlined design onto artist's tracing paper.

Choose a thread for the outline and thread the machine. Set the machine for a short stitch length. You can sew around twice or use a heavier thread if you want to emphasize the outline. You will need a small amount of cotton or synthetic stuffing or batting, a pushing tool such as a metal nail file, and a large sewing needle.

 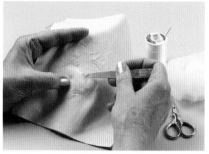

1 Sew along the lines of the design. This bunny was outlined in metallic thread. Remove the tracing paper after sewing.

2 On the back, with a sharp-pointed embroidery scissors, make a slash behind each sewn area. Do this carefully so you don't cut into the right side fabric. Push stuffing into each area using a pushing tool, working it so it is even. Use very small amounts for small areas. Use a large sewing needle to work the stuffing into narrow and small areas. By hand, sew each slash closed.

Insets

Insets were sewn as openings for bells and for setting in a lace motif.

This method adds little "windows" to a patch. Use it highlight a piece of lace, a photo transfer, or other image or motif. If you use lace or a motif, place fabric behind it. An inset can be sewn on plain fabric, or on a block that has a foundation layer.

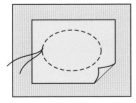

1 Lay a second fabric face down onto the base fabric, and stitch the shape of the opening such as a circle or oval.

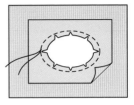

2 Cut out the center leaving a seam allowance of about ¼". Clip the seam allowance all around.

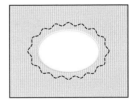

3 Push the second fabric to the back and press. Add a fabric-backed motif, lace, or other object of your choice behind the opening and tack it in place. Work some decorative embroidery around the finished inset.

Shaped-edge Patches

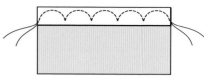

1 Lay a second fabric face down along the edge of a patch and sew scallops, curves, or zigzags.

2 Trim and clip the seam.

There's never a dull moment with crazy quilting. Even your patches can have fancy edges. After you put them onto a quilt, tack them down with embroidering a silk ribbon flower on each scallop, or sewing a button on each zigzag.

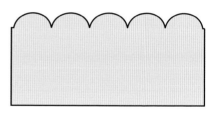

3 Turn the second fabric to the back and press. Add the patch to a crazy quilt.

Self-made Fringe

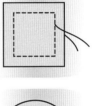

Cut a strip of fabric either on the straight grain or bias. Set the machine to a short stitch length and sew to the quilt top along the center of the strip. If you need to pre-mark the center before sewing, fold the strip in half lengthwise and press. Sew along the crease.

This is a simple idea that adds a softening touch. A fine, silk fabric will result in a delicate, wispy fringe. Heavier fabrics will make coarser fringes. These can be decorated after they are sewn onto a quilt top by embroidering along the sewn centers. They can be placed along patch edges, or meandered across patches.

There are two ways to make a fringe and each gives different results. Cut the strip on the straight grain of the fabric, sew, then ravel it almost to the stitching. This makes a "thready" fringe. Or, cut the strip on the bias, sew, then run the edges through your fingernails. This makes a slightly thready, wavy edge.

To make a thicker fringe, use two or more strips of fabric as one.

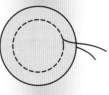

Pretty much the same way, cut out small squares or circles of fabric, sew them on and fray the edges. Sew on a quantity to decorate a patch center.

Styles of Crazy Quilts

A Thousand Stitches combines several concepts that are covered on the following pages: whole-quilt center, block-style border, checkerboard sashing, corner block fans, and edges finished with a binding.

Your patching method is a determinant in the style of a quilt. Machine methods, for instance, are easier to do on smaller areas, so blocks are the answer. The Antique method lends itself to large areas, making the whole-quilt style appropriate. Strip-patching creates bands that can be sewn vertically or in other directions.

Other aspects of quilt design involve dividing the quilt top into areas separated by sashings, using pieced fans in various ways, and whether to add a border. These elements not only determine how the area of the quilt top is used, but they are important to the decor of the quilt as well. Borders, for instance, can be patchwork or treated to appliqué, embroidery, or other design work. Working embroidery on sashings softens them and adds to the detail of the quilt.

Browse through this section, then sketch some of your own quilt ideas. Putting outlines on paper will help you to visualize a finished quilt. Decide how large you want the quilt, then figure what size to make each area. Add an amount of seam allowance for sewing the pieces together. Cut out foundation fabric for each piece. Even if a piece is not crazy patched, it should be backed with the same foundation fabric as the patched areas so all parts will be more equal to each other.

The parts of a quilt can be sewn together after blocks are patched and before embroidery, or after the blocks are completely finished. It all depends on how you prefer to work. After the quilt top is assembled, consider working a line of embroidery along each seam. This helps the seams to blend and is an opportunity to work meandering vines with leaves and silk ribbon flowers.

Block Style

Blocks divide a quilt top into manageable portions. The blocks for a quilt top can be made square or rectangular, large or small. Mix block sizes in a quilt, or make them all the same size.

There is no standard block size. Some people find 6" square blocks too small to work on, while others thrive on small areas. You will have to find what works best for you.

A perceived drawback of this style (for some) is that the quilt appears to consist of blocks. And why not, if it is? If you wish to conceal this fact, leave some patches hanging at the edges and appliqué them onto the adjoining block after blocks are sewn together. Or, elegantly blend them by working lines of embroidery over the seams.

Seam Allowance

Use a seam allowance that you are comfortable with, and that is in scale with the project. I usually use ¼" for a miniature quilt, and ½" for a larger piece and for most non-quilt projects. If a wider allowance creates too much fabric in the seam, it can always be trimmed back after sewing.

Pressing Seams

With heavier fabrics and patched foundations, pressing seams open prevents excessive bulk. It's usually best to press a seam open if you will be working embroidery along it.

Take-up

Take-up is the bunching that can occur as embroidery or other work is done. It can often be prevented. In patching or piecing, press carefully and check that the foundation is staying flat. In embroidery and embellishing use a hoop for hand work, and stabilizer for machine work. Some fabrics such as velveteen tend to crawl. This can be minimized by basting across in several directions. If, no matter what you do bunching still occurs, then cut your foundations larger to account for it.

Whole-Quilt Style

The whole-quilt style pairs well with hand patching methods such as the Antique and the Landscape methods. Unlike dividing the quilt top into blocks, the whole quilt style is worked as one unit and finishes as one. This presents an incredible opportunity to not only view the quilt as a landscape-like entity, but also to work on the whole piece at once. This changes the work order. Instead of completing a block at a time, a larger area evolves more gradually as one unit.

Possible patterns of embellishment distribution across a whole-quilt top.

Strips

Strips are bands running part or all the length or width of a quilt. They can be placed horizontally, vertically, or diagonally. Strips result naturally from the Strip Patching method (see page 32), but can be made using any other patching method as well. Use them exclusively, or combine them with blocks or sashings.

Sashings

Sashings are narrow strips of plain fabric 1" to 3" wide. Use them to keep blocks or strips separate from each other. Make sure the width of

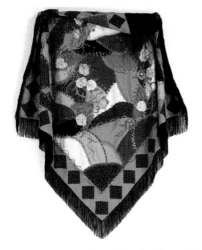

Note that the whole quilt style allows the top to become a one-unit composition.

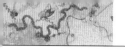

the sashings is appropriate for the quilt. Sashings can be patchwork as in the quilt, A Thousand Stitches.

Borders

Borders add to the size of a quilt and are an opportunity besides. Many antique crazy quilts use this area for embroideries. Borders can be done in patchwork, embroidered, appliquéd, or embellished in any number of ways.

See Finishing a Quilt (page 243) for instructions for borders.

Fans

Fans are very attractive on crazy quilts, and many antique crazies feature various types of them. A quilt can be designed around the use of fans. Sewing pieced fans is on page 169.

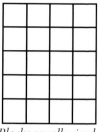

Blocks equally sized.

Blocks of various sizes.

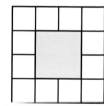

Blocks with a larger center focus block.

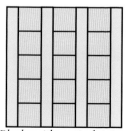

Blocks with vertical strips.

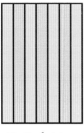

Vertical strips.

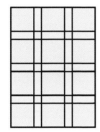

Blocks with sashings.

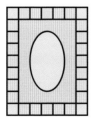

Block style border with oval center.

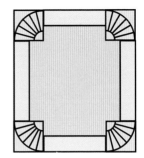

Place a fan at each corner of the border.

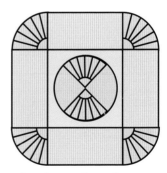

*Place fans at the quilt center.
Use them to shape the corners of a quilt.*

Finishing a Quilt

This exquisite antique crazy quilt is made in the Block Style with a plain border. Some of the blocks feature large embroidered patches. Museum Collection, Dyer Library/Saco Museum, Saco, Maine.

Read through this section before deciding what is the best way to finish your own quilt. If you are adding a border, what style will it be? Will the quilt be finished with a knife-edge or a binding? Are you adding a lace or ruffle to the edging?

A border is optional. If you don't want to have a border, finish a quilt top using the knife-edge finish on page 241, or bindings on page 245.

A border itself can be finished either with the knife edge finish, or with bindings.

If the borders are plain, choose a color that enhances the quilt. The width of the border should also enhance the quilt. To find an appropriate width, lay the quilt on the border fabric with an even amount peeking out. Adjust this until the width looks right for the quilt.

Yardage for Borders

A border should be cut all in one piece if at all possible. If the borders are short enough, cut them along the width of the fabric. For longer borders, use the length of the fabric.

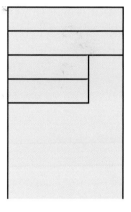

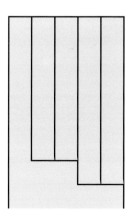

Plain Border

Instructions:

Follow these instructions for any of the border styles below:

- Add seam allowances to each border piece or corner block.

- Border seams are normally pressed toward the border, but can be pressed open to make it easier to embroider along them.

- For the quilt to hang properly, back each border piece with the same fabric used for the quilt foundation and handle the two fabrics as one.

- After the borders are sewn onto the quilt top, work any embroidery desired, either along the border or along the sewn seams. Then add a backing.

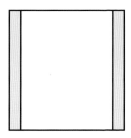

1 Measure the length of the quilt top. Cut two borders this length and sew them on.

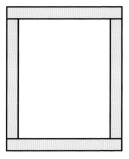

2 Measure the quilt's width, including the two side borders. Cut two borders this length. Sew one to the top, and the other to the bottom of the quilt.

*This antique crazy quilt has a velvet border with contrasting corner blocks.
The daisy petals are embroidered in ribbon. Detail. Museum Collection,
Dyer Library/Saco Museum, Saco, Maine.*

Border with Corner Blocks

Make same as the Plain Border
except cut two borders the same
length, and two the same width as
the quilt top.

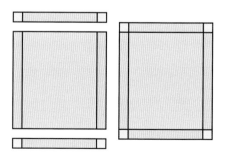

1 Sew on the side borders.

2 Make four corner blocks. Sew one
to each end of the top and bottom
borders, then sew to the quilt top.

Border with Mitered Corners

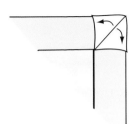

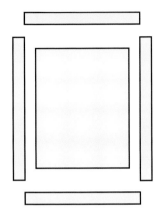

1 Cut two borders each the length of the quilt top plus two border widths. Cut two borders each the width of the quilt top plus two border widths

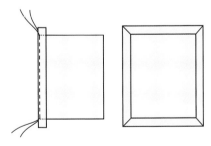

2 Sew on all of the borders, centering them on the quilt. Do not sew into the seam allowances at each end.

3 Place one corner of the quilt on the ironing board. Fold back the two adjoining borders and press a diagonal crease in each. Repeat for each corner.

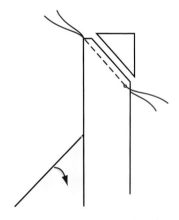

4 One corner at a time, with right sides together and the quilt folded diagonally, line up the two creases, pin, and sew from the outer to the inner edge. Trim off the excess fabric and press the seam open.

Backing

Plain cotton fabrics make appropriate backings for many quilts. If you want to go a step better, use cotton sateen. It has a beautiful sheen. This fabric was often used for lining vests and backing crazy quilts in the old days.

An all-silk quilt should be backed with silk especially if the quilt has a silk batting. Use a plain woven silk fabric.

If the quilt is sewn with a knife-edge finish (see page 241), consider that the backing will show right at the edges (unless a ruffle, lace, or fringe is used). You might choose a color that blends with the quilt top, or daringly pick a contrasting color that will show as a sliver at the edges.

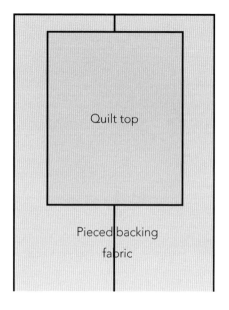

Make the backing the same size as the top, including any borders. Piece the fabric as necessary. Seams on pieced backings should be vertical and centered.

Batting

Stabilizing Heavily Embellished Quilts

Quilt tops that have become heavy due to the objects sewn to them require special treatment in the finishing. First, see what can be done about avoiding excess weight in the planning stages of the quilt. Silk trims, for example, weigh next to nothing compared to cottons and rayons. French knots add a dotty effect and can be done in glossy rayon thread instead of sewing on lots of glass beads, and so on.

But if your quilt top has become heavy some steps can be taken to prevent sagging that can occur when the quilt is hung. Add a layer of sturdy interfacing behind the foundation fabric and tack it on in many places or use long random basting stitches into the foundation but not through to the front. Look for a heavyweight non-woven interfacing, or use hair canvas or some other type of stiff fabric. Add the backing on top of that, and tie as usual (see page 243). Bind the edges of the quilt (see page 215).

Most often, the foundation substitutes for batting in a crazy quilt. If you want to add a batting, however, choose one that can be tied 6" to 8" apart. If you've chosen natural fibers for your quilting fabrics (cotton, linens, rayons, silks, etc), you may also want to chose a natural batting such as cotton or wool.

A silk batting is often desirable in a silk quilt for extra loft especially if silk organza is used for the foundation, because organza is very thin. There are different kinds of silk battings, from "caps" that are yanked and pulled on until they are stretched to the size needed, to those that resemble an ordinary batting. Follow the instructions that come with the batting.

Knife-Edge Finish

The Piano Shawl is made of drapey rayon challis fabrics and finished with a fringe sewn into a knife-edge border.

Bindings are eliminated if the quilt is sewn with right sides together to the backing and then turned right side out. Knife-edge quilts can have lace, a ruffle, or fringe sewn into the edge. See Gathering Lace and Making Ruffles on the following page.

1 If you are adding lace or trim, pin it to the quilt's edge with right sides together. Tuck a little extra into each corner. Overlap and bring lace or ruffle ends outward, butt fringe ends.

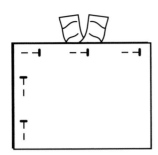

2 Place the backing on top with right sides together. If you are using a batting, place this on top of the backing. Pin through all layers.

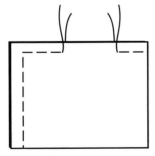

3 Sew around leaving an opening to turn. Trim corners, turn, press. Sew the opening closed. Finish the quilt by tying the layers. If the quilt is large, spread it out smooth and pin at intervals or baste to hold the layers. Then tie.

Gathering Lace and Making Ruffles

Laces with one long raw edge are intended to be sewn into a seam. Fabric laces such as eyelets fall into this category.

Ruffles for crazy quilts are especially luxurious in silk. Choose a lightweight silk fabric such a Habotai (China silk). Decide on the width of the ruffle and cut the fabric on the bias (see page 245) twice the width plus seam allowances. Sew the bias strips together to make one long piece. Fold this in half lengthwise and proceed as if it were one layer.

You will need lace or ruffle fabric that is at least 1½ times the circumference of the quilt.

1 Sew a long machine stitch along the unfinished edge of the ruffle or lace, and pull up on one thread to gather.

2 Continue with step 1 of the Knife-Edge Finish.

Note: If the ruffle is wide, sew its ends together (right sides together), and then pin to the quilt top, rather than overlapping the ends. This will make a neater finish.

Tying the Quilt

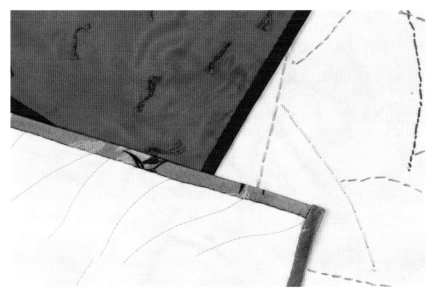

Three quilts, each finished differently. Tied with knotted silk embroidery thread, layers tied with French Knots on the front with the effect of running stitch on the back, and quilted randomly by machine.

Crazy quilts are traditionally tied, not quilted. There are many ways to tie a quilt. Ties can be "hidden" or used to decorate the quilt surface, on the front or the back. They can be individual ties, or embroidery stitches.

Make individual ties using doubled or a single strand of pearl cotton. Sew several at once by making stitches a few inches apart. Snip the thread between stitches and tie a square knot in each.

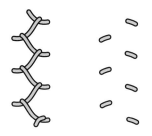

*The front and back of the Feather Stitch
used for tying a quilt.*

Work individual embroidery stitches
such as French Knots close together
so the thread runs only a short ways
on the back of the quilt. Continuous
stitches such as Feather Stitch or
Cretan Stitch will make little "tracks"
on the back of the quilt.

Or, try a neat but "sneaky" way
to use embroidery stitches as ties.
This is done by running the needle
through fabric layers for a ways, then
stopping to make a French Knot or
other stitch through all of the layers.
Fasten the embroidery thread by
making several tiny stitches under the
edge of a patch on the surface of the
quilt to avoid fastenings that show on
the back.

Individual ties on the back of a quilt
can be concealed with small bows.
Use ribbon about ½" wide, tie a bow,
and tack it on.

Bindings

Silk dupioni binding finishes the edges of this silk quilt.

Completely finish the quilt top including any borders and tie the layers. Traditionally, bindings are made of cotton or cotton blend fabrics, but you can use any fabric that works. If the quilt is square or rectangular, the binding can be cut along the straight grain of the fabric. If there are curved edges, make a bias binding.

strips 2¼". The extra quarter inch allows for the thickness of the quilt. If you find this too wide, cut the strips 1⅞" or 2⅛" wide.

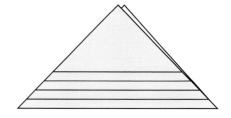

Making Bias Binding

Begin with a yard or so of fabric. The width to cut the bindings depends on the desired finished width. A finished width of ¼" requires 1¼". For the binding to finish to ½" wide, cut the

1 Fold the fabric in half diagonally, press the folded edge, then cut along the fold.

2 Cut the bias strips using a rotary cutter, cutting mat, and acrylic ruler.

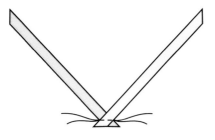

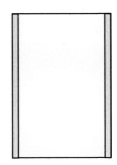

3 Place two strips with right sides together and sew the seam. Press the seam to one side. Continue, joining the strips until you have the length needed.

2 Press each binding to the back and press the long unsewn edge under.

3 Slipstitch each binding to the quilt backing, covering the seam.

Sew on the Bindings

4 Sew one binding to the top and one to the bottom edge of the quilt leaving ½" extra binding at each end.

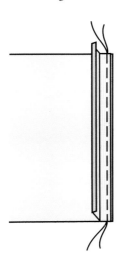

1 Sew one to each side edge of the quilt.

5 Press to the back, press the long edge under, and clean finish the corners. Slipstitch.

Appendix

Fiber Types

Following is a basic run-down of the most common natural fibers. Whether as embroidery threads or fabrics, the natural fibers are recommended for their ease of handling, surface texture, and characteristics such as dyeability, comfort, weight, and so on. As fabrics, most of the fibers are available in a wide range of weaves, giving the quilter much to choose from.

Do not confuse fibers with weaves. Satin, for instance, is not a fiber but a weave that creates "floats" of threads on the surface of the fabric. The floats catch the light, making the surface appear lustrous. Satin fabric can be made of silk, acetate, or cotton. Each of these is a different fabric in characteristics such as weight, drape, and surface luster.

Cotton

Cotton comes from the seed cases (bolls) of the cotton plant. Some cotton fabrics and threads are treated to a mercerization process (immersion in caustic soda) which straightens the fiber, imparts luster, and gives it greater strength and better affinity for dyes. Weaves range from coarse

Wool crazy quilts have a charm of their own, and were often more useful than decorative. Detail. Museum Collection, Dyer Library/Saco Museum, Saco, Maine.

or plain fabrics such as muslin, lawn, and canvas to napped fabrics such as flannel (one-sided or two), corduroy, terry cloth, and velveteen. Fancier weaves include sateen (satin weave), damask (woven-in patterns), laces, and others.

Cotton can take high temperatures in both washing and ironing. It dyes easily. The fiber is breathable making it ideal for comfortable clothing and quilts.

Cotton fabrics and embroidery threads are the easiest to work with and are recommended for beginners.

Silk

Silk is a natural protein fiber made from the cocoons of silkworms. Spun silk is silk thread made by spinning short fibers. Filament silk, considered to be of higher quality, is made by unreeling a silk cocoon to produce one long fiber.

Silk fabrics include the plain weaves: China silk (also known as Habotai), organza, broadcloth and others. Noil and dupioni are plain woven also, but have texture due to the uneven qualities of their threads. Fancier silk types include crepe, satin, jacquard (woven-in patterns), and others.

Silk is the strongest of the natural fibers and has an inherent luster. It is the most prized of fibers, and often used in haute couture. It drapes exceptionally, is lightweight and comfortable to wear, and makes the most luxurious of quilts.

Silks are highly absorbent, and are easy to dye. Wash in cool to lukewarm water using mild soap or a natural shampoo. Roll in a towel to absorb excess water, and line dry. Press using steam.

Linen

Linen is made from the fibers of the flax plant. It is stronger than cotton, and has a unique and subtle luster. Fabrics made from it tend to be either plain woven or damask (woven-in patterning). They vary from the very lightweight handkerchief linens, to heavy canvas. Some linens are slubbed, and others entirely smooth. Linens make excellent embroidery backgrounds, and you can find them in evenweaves for working cross stitch, or plain weaves for crewel embroidery.

Linen fabrics make wonderful patches on a crazy quilt.

Linen is lint free, very washable at any temperature, highly absorbent, and easy to dye. It also wrinkles easily. Iron it while damp using a high temperature.

Wool

Wool is a hair fiber coming from sheep or other fleece such as alpaca, camel, mohair (from the angora goat), or angora (from the Angora rabbit). With the popularity of hand spinning, dog hair, yak hair, and other fibers have also been made into threads. Very little processing is needed besides carding or combing the fiber before spinning it, although commercial processes are more complex.

Fabric types include challis, suitings, blanketings, and others. The lighter weights of wool fabrics make excellent patches on a crazy quilt, or use them to make a wool crazy quilt.

Wool is very washable but will shrink and felt if mishandled. To wash, add a mild soap to cool to lukewarm water and allow the wool to soak without agitation. Rinse, also by soaking, using the same water temperature. Change the rinse water until it stays clear. Roll in a towel to absorb excess water. Dry flat or supported away from any heat sources, sun included, otherwise it is likely to shrink.

Rayon

Rayon was created in an attempt to make artificial silk in the late 1800's with the process being reinvented several times until a useful fiber came of it. The process first liquifies wood fiber, then creates filaments that are then turned back into cellulose.

Types include matte to very shiny surfaces. Fabric types include the drapey challis (perfect for appliqué and for making drapey quilts), to many home decorating types and velveteen.

Rayon is highly absorbent, comfortable to wear, and dyes easily. It weakens when wet, but firms up upon drying. Straighten kinky rayon threads by dampening them, and allow to dry before using. Wash gently in cool to lukewarm water. Do not wring or twist. Hang to dry and press while damp using a moderate heat setting.

Displaying and Storing Quilts

An important step upon finishing a quilt is to make sure it has some documentation. A monogram and the year the quilt was finished are standard ways to sign and date a crazy quilt (see Monograms on page 173).

If there are interesting details about your life and the making of the quilt, write them down. Sew a small pocket to the backing to store this information. If you don't know what to write, go to see a beautiful Victorian crazy quilt in a museum. Wonder who the maker was and what her life was like. This tells you what to write—tell the onlooker of 100 years from now what she wants to know about your quilt. Any writing whether on or with the quilt should be done in permanent ink so no matter what happens, the ink cannot run into the quilt.

Hang a Quilt:

- Out of sunlight on a wall that sunshine never touches
- Safely away from any fumes, smoke, or cooking
- Not touching the wall

Make enough quilts so you can periodically change the quilt on display. One for each season, or one per month... (keep on quilting!).

Quilts used on a bed or as afghans should be washable or dry cleanable and do not require any special handling. A cleanable quilt must begin with prewashing or pre-dry-cleaning all fabrics going into it, and checking that trims and threads are cleanable also. It's wonderful to have quilts that can be used. They do wear out eventually, and I call that an opportunity for a future project.

Antique and heirloom quilts are a different story, and should be handled only with clean cotton gloves to avoid oils and microscopic dirt getting on the quilt. Having watched unknowing friends run up to a displayed quilt and grab handfuls of it, I now know to speak up quickly and say that show quilts are not handled.

To clean the quilt, vacuum without touching the surface. If the vacuum is powerful, cut down on the suction and/or place a piece of nylon stocking over the hose so nothing gets sucked in. I like to air my quilts outdoors on a warm breezy, non-humid day and they seem to love this—they come in smelling fresh and clean. Do not put any quilt in the sunshine.

To store a quilt, wrap in clean cloth and store it in a dry place. It is best to keep an heirloom quilt in an acid free box. Get the quilt out once or twice a year and refold it in a different way. This helps prevent damage along fold lines. You can use acid-free tissue paper or clean cotton cloth to pad the folds, especially if the quilt is heavily embellished.

About the Author

J. Marsha Michler is author of eleven books, including *The Magic of Crazy Quilting, Crazy Quilts by Machine, Crazy Quilted Heirlooms and Gifts, Motifs for Crazy Quilting*, and *Crazy Quilt Décor* from Krause Publications. She has written many articles and projects for magazines, and has won quilt awards for her crazy quilts. Marsha actively pursues various other needlearts, jewelry making, spinning, knitting, crocheting, pottery, photography, and website design. In her spare time she gardens, builds stone walls, travels, and enjoys sushi with her husband. She resides in the beautiful foothills of southern Maine.

Sources

Website; project instructions, links page:

J. Marsha Michler

www.jmarshamichler.com

Artemis Exquisite Embellishments

5155 Myrtle Ave., Eureka, CA 95503

1-888-233-5187   www.artemisinc.com

Silk bias-cut ribbons,

colorfast hand-dyeds in 5 widths

The Button Drawer

6844 S. Franklin Circle, Centennial, CO 80122

info@buttondrawer.com   www.buttondrawer.com

Buttons

The Caron Collection

203-381-9999

mail@caron-net.com   www.caron-net.com

Waterlilies, Wildflowers, Watercolours, and

Kit Kin

Dharma Trading Co.

P.O. Box 150916, San Rafael, CA 94915

1-800-542-5227

www.dharmatrading.com

Marbling supplies, silk fabrics,

paints, and dyes

The DMC Corporation

77 South Hackensack Ave., Bldg. 10F

South Kearny, NJ 07032

973-589-0606   www.dmc-usa.com

Pearl Cotton, Light Effects threads

Fire Mountain Gems

1 Fire Mountain Way, Grants Pass, OR 97526-2373

1-800-355-2137   www.firemountaingems.com

Beads and beading supplies

Gloriana Threads

15410 NE 157th Street, Woodinville, WA 98072

425-488-0479   www.glorianathreads.com

Hand-dyed silk perle threads and silk ribbons

Kreinik Mfg. Co., Inc.

1708 Gihon Rd., Parkersburg, WV 26102

1-800-537-2166   www.kreinik.com

Silk Serica, Silk Bella, Metallic braids, ribbons,

threads, and Gold and Silver Japan threads

Lacis

3163 Adeline St., Berkeley, CA 94703

510-843-7178   www.lacis.com

Lace-making supplies

Laura Murray Designs

www.lauramurraydesigns.com

Foiling, stencils and rubbing supplies

Newark Dressmaker

P.O. Box 4099, Bethlehem, PA 18018

800-736-6783   www.newarkdress.com

Laces, trims, threads and general supplies

Piecemakers Country Store

1720 Adams Avenue, Costa Mesa, CA 92626

714-641-3112   www.piecemakers.com

Embroidery, Sharps, Milliner's, and Chenille hand sewing needles

Rupert, Gibbon and Spider, Inc.

P.O. Box 425, Healdsburg, CA 95448

800-442-0455   www.jacquardproducts.com

Paints, dyes, silks, and inkjet fabrics

Thai Silks

252 State Street, Los Altos, CA 94022

800-722-7455   www.thaisilks.com

Silk fabrics

Things Japanese

9805 NE 116 St., PMB 7160

Kirkland, WA 98034-2287

425-821-2287   www.silkthings.com

Colorhue dyes, silk ribbons, and Tire silk threads

ThreadArt

13529-N Skinner Rd., Cypress, TX 77429

800-504-6867   www.threadart.com

100% cotton sewing thread, dupioni silk (hand woven), and muslin

Victoria Clayton

6448 Freeman Rd., Byron, NY 14422

585-494-8342

vikki@hand-dyedfbers.com

www.hand-dyedfibers.com

Hand-dyed silk ribbons and silk perle threads

Yodama, Inc.

13502 Airport Cutoff Rd.

Port Townsend, WA 98368-9320

866-334-3085   www.eternasilk.com

Eterna silk threads

YLI Corp.

1439 Dave Lyle Blvd. #16C

Rock Hill, SC 29730-4295

803-985-3106 (phone and fax)

www.ylicorp.com

Pearl Crown Rayon Thread, 1000 denier silk thread, silk ribbon, and 100% cotton quilting threads

Index